THE ...

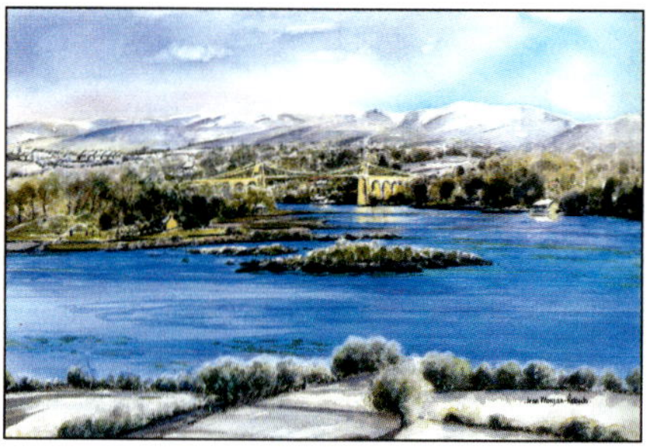

The Character of Conwy

Jean Morgan-Roberts

In Memory of my father,
William Henry Morgan
who loved the Black Lion

ISBN: 1-84524-072-3
978-184524-072-1

Cover design: Sian Parri

First published in 2007 by
Llygad Gwalch, Ysgubor Plas, Llwyndyrys, Pwllheli, Gwynedd
Wales LL53 6NG.
Phone: 01758 750432
e-mail: gai@llygadgwalch.com
Website: www.llygadgwalch.com

Contents

Foreword	6
Porth Uchaf	7
St Mary's and All Saints Church	8
The musselmen of Conwy	10
Aberconwy House	12
The Smallest House in Great Britain	14
Plas Mawr	16
Keith Robinson	18
Llangelynnin old church	20
David Thomas Jones	22
Hafoty	24
Cymryd	26
Conwy Castle	28
The Black Lion	30
Sir Kyffin Williams	32
Peggy Rowlands	34
Margaret Williams	36
Michael Senior	38
Keith Robinson	40
Ivor Peris Roberts	42
Hugh Roberts	44
Betty Pattinson	46
David Gwynfor Price	48
Peter McFadden	50
Tom Morris	52
Doctor Geoff Moore	54
Peter Hugh John	56
Raymond Hughes	58
Ken Rimmer Hughes	60
Bryn Hughes	62
Tony Tobin	64
Lord John Roger Roberts	66
Lord Roberts of Conwy	68
Jean Morgan-Roberts	70
Jane Hardy	72
George Edwards	74
Edward Doylerush	76
Dennis Wright	78

Foreword

Jean Morgan-Roberts was born in the Black Lion, which had been a 16th century vicarage, thus entitling her to membership of the Jackdaw Society, an exclusive club for those born within the town walls of Conwy.

She started drawing and painting when she was 11, concentrating mainly on birds. In the early autumn of 1956 she left Conwy to live in Liverpool and on the Wirral. On her return to Wales she found people wanted paintings of Conwy and she sold them at markets and agricultural shows and on the pavement on Rhos-on-Sea. Her talent came to the attention of firms specialising in calendars, Christmas cards and postcards and she travelled all over the country to paint picturesque scenes. Soon she had her own shop almost opposite her old home.

Jean has travelled extensively in her search for fresh subjects and spent some time in Patagonia. She is married to Ivor Peris Roberts and they live locally near their children.

Now she exhibits pictures of places she has seen in various parts of the world, but finds the Conwy views are what local people and visitors want most. She has exhibited at most art venues and galleries on the northern Wales coast and a lot of her work can be seen in hotels, breweries, hospitals, bars and restaurants. People from all parts of the world have shipped her work abroad.

Quite an achievement for someone who has never been to art school.

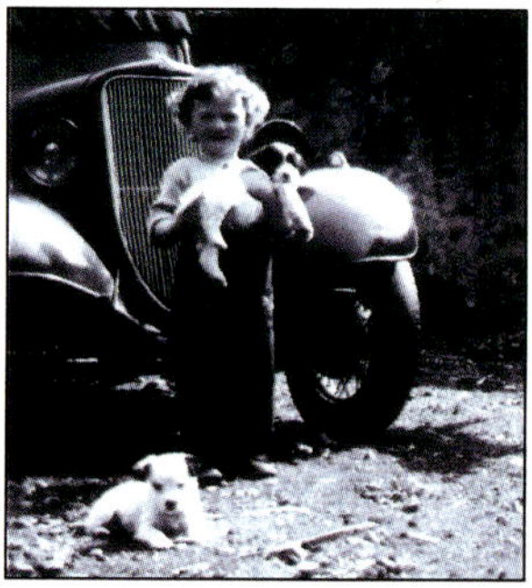

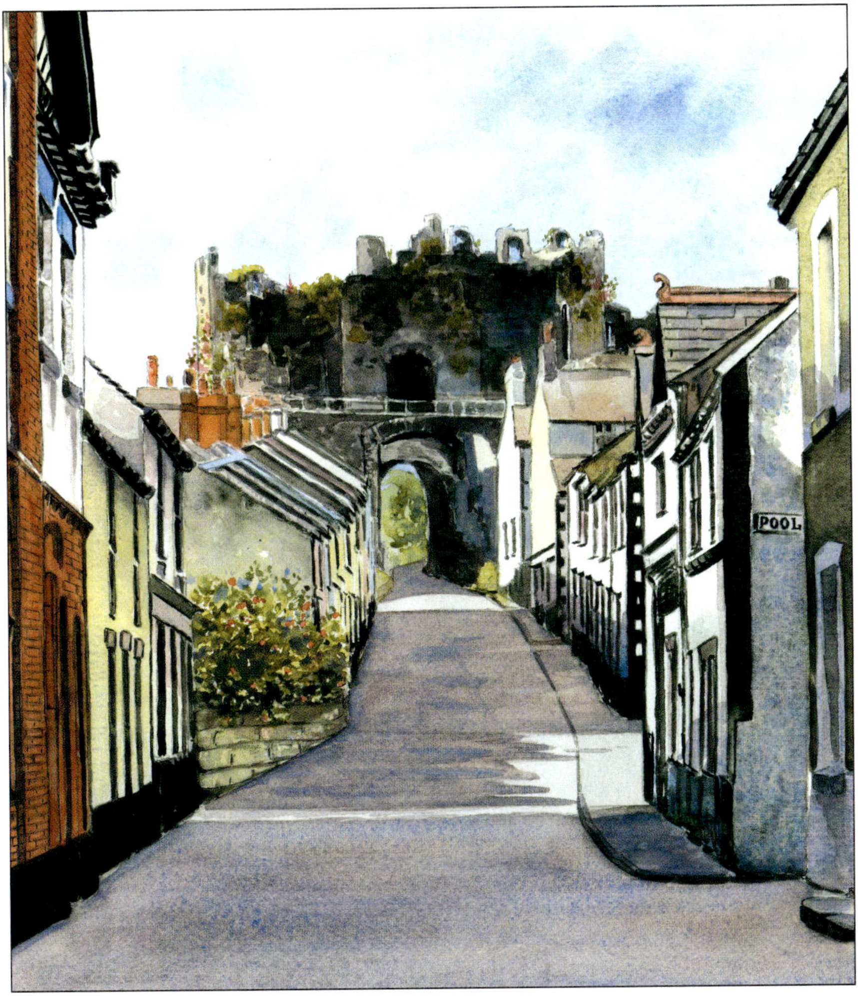

Porth Uchaf

The Upper Gate – once upon a time, the main gate of the town through which all traffic passed. The road ahead leads to the Sychnant Pass and Dwygyfylchi.

St Mary's and All Saints' Church

Conwy parish church, dedicated to St Mary and All Saints, was originally a Cistercian abbey whose foundation was marked out in 1172 AD.

Completed in 1186, the abbey was formally incorporated into the Cistercian order the following year and in 1198 Llywelyn the Great granted a charter confirming the gifts and privileges he had bestowed on it.

The abbey was a depository for Welsh national records and public acts and was also renowned for its library. It also became a mausoleum for native princes, for among those buried there were Gruffydd ap Cynan, Llywelyn ap Maelgwn, Llywelyn the Great and his sons Dafydd and Gruffudd. Llywelyn the Great's body was later removed to Maenan and then to Llanrwst church where the coffin is still to be seen.

In 1245 the English army, under Henry III, raided the abbey and burnt a number of the buildings surrounding it and removed its chalices and books. Then, in 1283, Edward I thought the noise of construction would harm the peaceful lives of the monks so he gave them land at Maenan where they remained until the Dissolution, and St Mary's then became the parish church.

The east and west end buttresses and parts of the north wall have survived from the original 12th century church. In the 14th century, lower stages of the tower, south transept and porches were erected. The tower was completed, the rood screen and font were erected by the 15th century.

The church contains many interesting features. There is a marble bust of John Gibson, the sculptor, who was baptised in the church in 1790. In the south aisle is an effigy of Mary, mother of John Williams, Archbishop of York and Keeper of the Great Seal of England. In the chancel is a 17th century floor slab inscribed Nicholas Hookes, the 41st child of his father and himself father to 27 children. A reproduction of Andrea del Sarto's 'Christ' is near the pulpit.

The rood screen, one of the finest in northern Wales, represents 15th century craftsmen at their best. A unique Tudor font has a moulded octagonal base with panels of the pedestal and bowl decorated with tracery. John Williams was baptised here on March 17, 1582.

The Cross is of early Byzantine workmanship, probably used in Monza cathedral, Italy, from the 7th to the 18th centuries for the procession of archbishops.

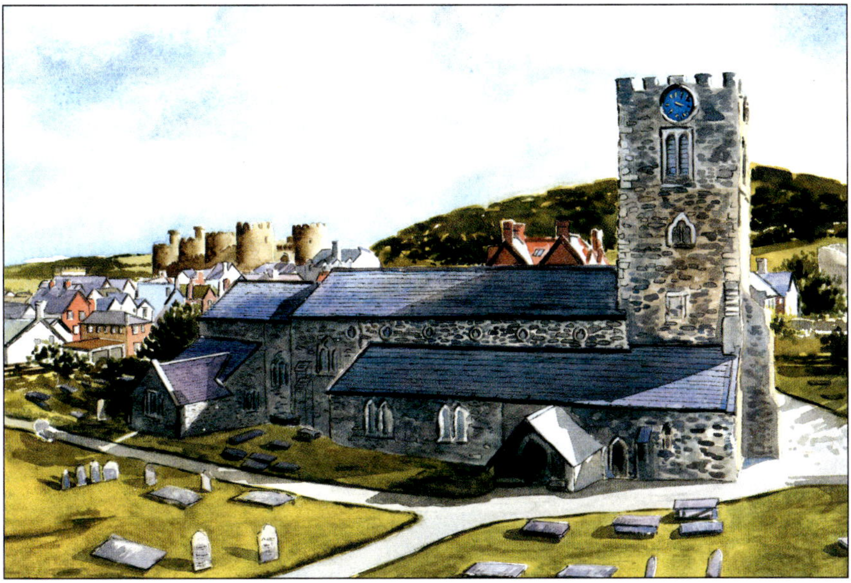

The musselmen of Conwy

Conwy's oldest industry, that of mussel fishing, began in the twelfth century when a group of Cistercian monks came to this country from France and established their abbey here at Aberconwy, the mouth of the river. The Cistercians always built their houses far from the haunts of men, which indicates that Conwy was a lonely place, a far cry from the bustling town it became over the years.

The monks invented the long rakes which the musselmen use to this day and here they taught those living by the river how to earn their living from gathering the blue shellfish.

The mussel beds are now protected by law to aid conservation. The season is from September to April, leaving the mussels to breed during the summer months.

Mussels grow close together, attaching themselves to rocks, stones and one another by their byssus threads.

Sometimes pearls are found inside the shells of mussels, although these days they are incredibly tiny ones. A far cry from the time when a pearl from the river found its way into the Crown Jewels. It was given to Sir Richard Wynne of Gwydir, who was chamberlain to Catherine, consort of King Charles II, and he duly went to court to present it to Her Majesty.

Pearls were so plentiful then that there was a special kitchen on the Morfa, a small room of wattle and gorse with a hole in the roof for smoke to escape. Here the mussels were boiled, the shells crushed by barefooted children and the pearls put into little bags and taken to be sold in Chester where they fetched between six and twelve shillings an ounce.

The mussel industry has risen and fallen over the years. In 1929, according to earliest records, there were 55 mussel men and by 1939 there were 75. Now there are just 19.

Picture shows: Darren Hughes, Jamie Hughes, Martin Parry and Thomas Leaping sorting out their catch.

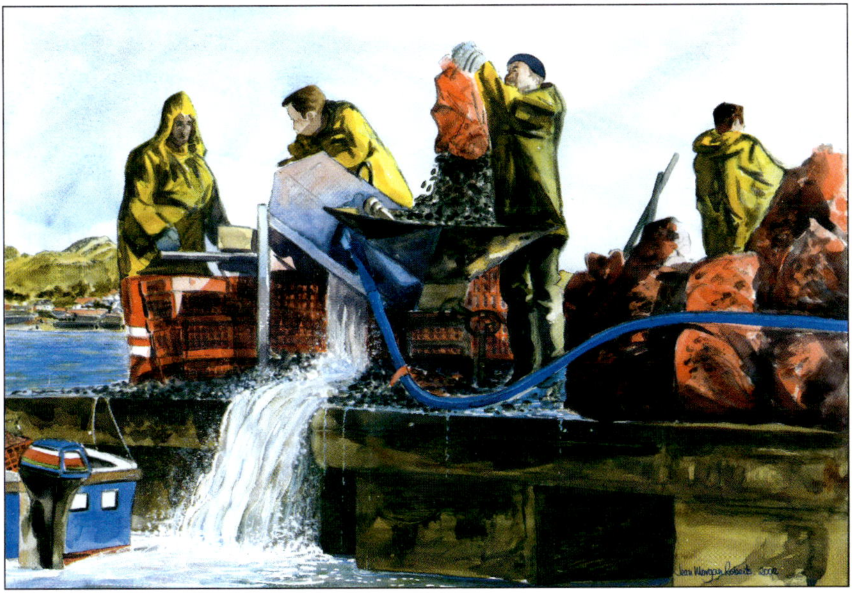

Aberconwy House

Aberconwy, the oldest house in Conwy – and said by some to be the oldest in Wales – stands on a site which was part of the grounds of the Cistercian monastery. When Edward I moved the monks to a new site at Maenan the road pattern of the town was laid out. English settlers were then invited to build their houses here with trade and tax concessions and plots of land being offered as inducements to enter this strange and hostile land.

The newcomers built houses on the individual brugages allotted to them, each being of a size to allow garden and orchard space around the house, for Conwy became known as a town noted for its floral displays.

While the names of most of the English families who settled here are well known, there is no indication of who lived at Aberconwy House but it must have been a merchant of some standing.

Over the years the house had many uses. In the 19th century it became a coffee house and temperance hotel, extending into the first two houses in High Street. The ground floor was a bakery and then the entire building became a museum and antique shop.

In 1934 the house was in danger of being taken down and shipped to the United States for re-erection and it was then that Mr Alexander Campbell Blair of Llandudno bought the building and gave it to the National Trust.

The National Trust started extensive repairs and renovations in 1976 and decided that the two upper floors should be devoted to the history of the walled town of Conwy while the ground floor should be a Trust shop.

In addition to essential strengthening of the fabric and the repair and renewal of the roof and structural timbers, it has been possible to expose the original timber framework of the upper storey and the old building has entered a further period of its illustrious life.

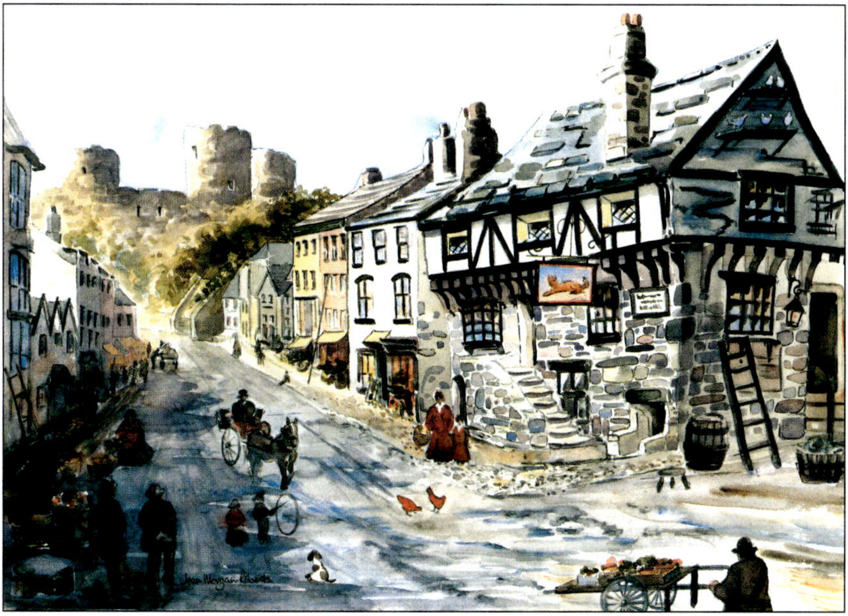

The Smallest House in Great Britain

One of the biggest attractions in Conwy. Occupied up till May 1900, its last tenant was, a 6 ft 3 inch fisherman named Robert Jones who rented the cottage for one shilling (5p) per week.

Since then countless people from all over the world have visited the tiny house and marvelled that it was actually lived in.

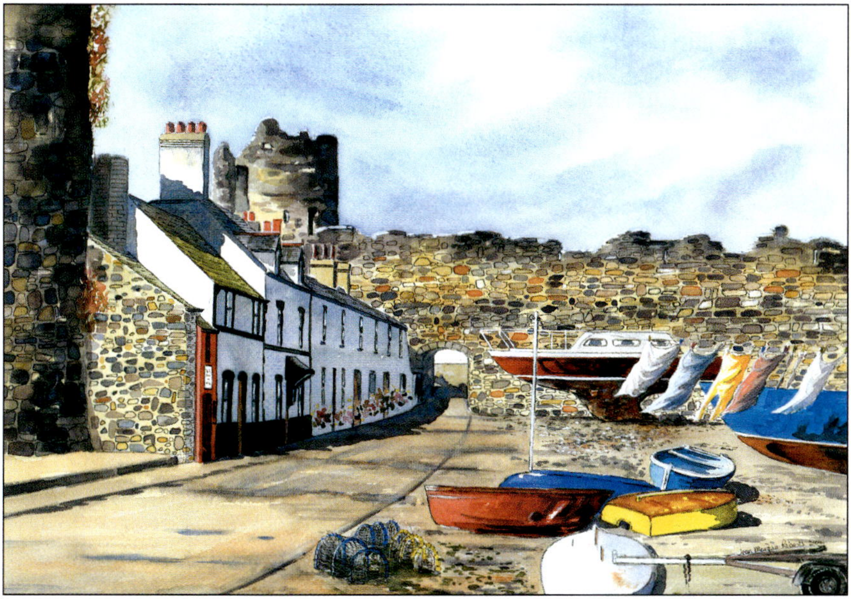

Plas Mawr

When Edward I created the town of Conwy no Welshman was allowed to build within the walls. This continued until the time of the Tudors and during the reign of Mary, Robert Wynne, the third son of John Wynne of Gwydir, retired to Conwy after a stirring, adventurous life, acquired land and built the fantastic mansion he called Plas Mawr which had 365 windows, 52 doors and 52 steps up to the tower.

His second son inherited Plas Mawr but because he was a Catholic had to relinquish the mansion because those of that faith were not allowed to hold property. The house and the estate then passed to his uncle, Hugh Wynne, and he and his descendants lived there until the end of the 17th century. One of the young women in the family became the heiress and she married into the Mostyns. The Mostyn family lived here for many years but then they deserted it.

Plas Mawr then fell on hard times. It was too large for anyone in Conwy to maintain it as a residence and so it was let out in tenements. Various little businesses were carried on by the tenants. There was a saddler in the cellar, a dairy man kept cows in the upper courtyard and for about 50 years the Conwy infants school occupied the reception room.

In 1887 the Royal Cambrian Academy of Art secured a lease from Lord Mostyn and had its permanent home there until, in 1993 Lord Mostyn placed Plas Mawr in the guardianship of the state. CADW: Welsh Historic Monuments took over the conservation of the house and now maintains it on behalf of the National Assembly of Wales.

CADW closed the house in order to carry out a programme of restoration and one of the tasks involved was bringing colour back to the ornate plaster decorations which had been whitewashed over during the austere days of the Civil War. Said by many to be among the most perfect specimens in Britain, these include royal arms and badges and the arms of the Wynne and Griffith families.

Plas Mawr was surrounded by gardens. The present entrance in High Street did not exist when the building first took shape and the main doorway was in Crown Lane with gardens sweeping down to the town wall. A truly magnificent sight.

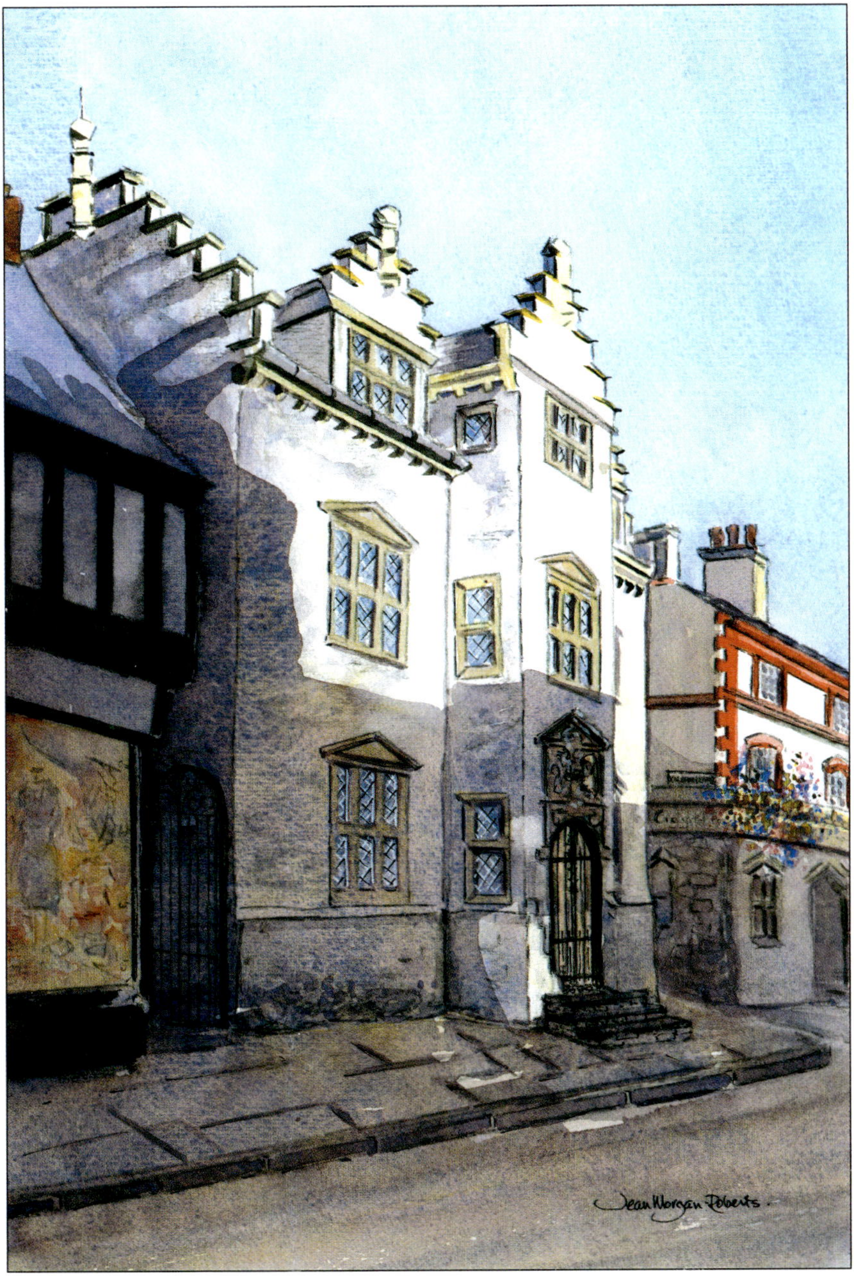
Jean Morgan Roberts.

Keith Robinson (Keith Fish)

One of Conwy's most well-known characters, Keith Robinson's surname was unknown to many. He was always 'Keith Fish', the man who sold the fruits of the sea from his stall at the end of the quay. For years Keith braved every kind of weather, shut only on Christmas Day, and was known to all the locals and countless visitors who came to the town every year.

Keith started his working life as an apprentice joiner but in his spare time helped his grandfather Tom Craven with his fish business on the quay where they sold ready boxed, iced fish which came from the trawlers. When Tom died Keith took over the stall and eventually upgraded to a kiosk where he traded for 40 years until his untimely death in 2005.

One of the founder members of the lifeboat crew when the station opened in 1966, he never failed to answer the call and neither bath, bed nor customers would interfere in this line of duty. He eventually became deputy launch authority and then honorary secretary and launch operation manager and was presented with a pair of binoculars by the RNLI for his services. Later he was awarded a gold badge for his dedication to duty and he and his wife Denise went to the Barbican Centre in London to accept the award.

His death left a gap which cannot be filled.

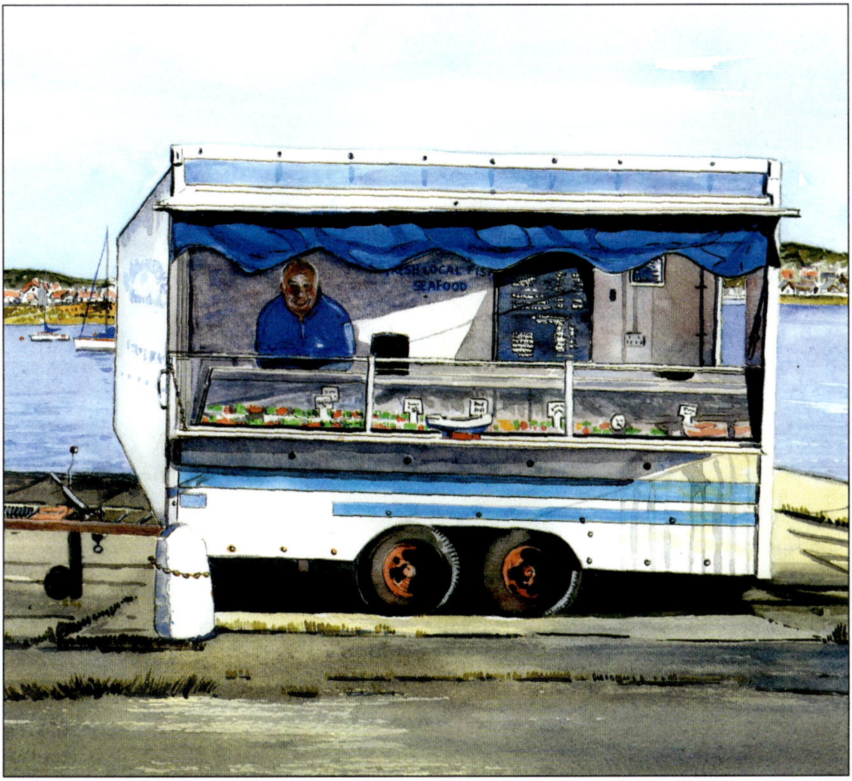
SEAFOOD

Llangelynnin old church

Nestling in the hollow of a mountain three miles from Conwy is the ancient church of Llangelynnin where countless people have worshipped since the seventh century.

Here, 927 feet above the sea, there is little sign of life save in the summer when hymns and psalms ring out over the valley. But it was not always like this.

A community once lived here and wrested a living from the rocky uplands and the stones on the hilly mounds are the remains of a cockpit and an inn.

The original church, dedicated to the seventh century saint Celynnin was probably made of wood. The oldest part of the present church is the nave which was built in the twelfth century. Parts were added over the years, the chancel was built in the fourteenth century, the east window, the porch and the north transept about a hundred years later, the latter being known as the Chapel of the Men when the sexes were separated in church.

Outside the church is a well where people would bring their sick children in the hope of a cure. The clothes of the children were thrown in and only if they floated was there any hope of recovery.

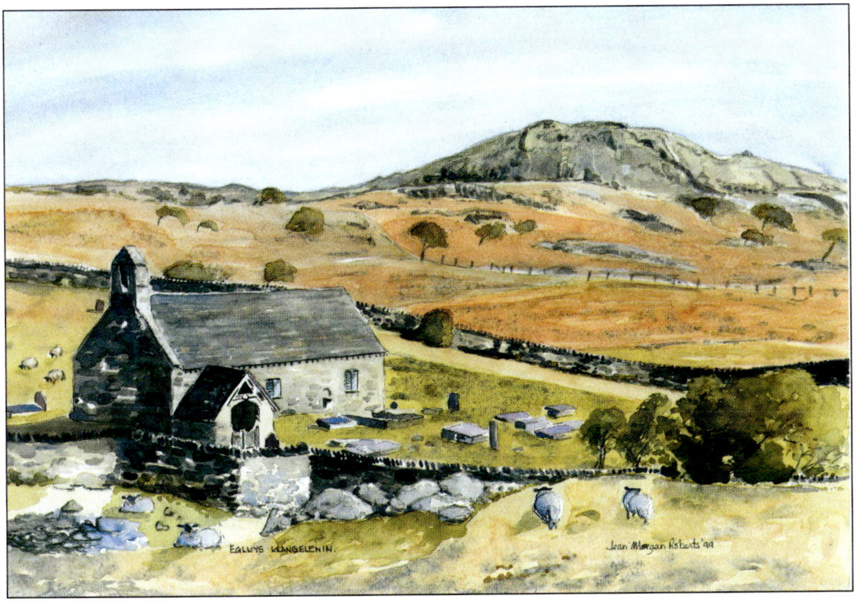
EGLWYS LLANGELENIN.
Jean Morgan Roberts '99

David Thomas Jones (Tom Hafoty)

David has lived at the foot of Tal-y-fan all his life and is the fifth generation of his family to farm Hafoty. He knows every inch of the mountain, every sheep in his own flock and every earmark denoting ownership of each flock that graze there. His life has been dedicated to the farm and its animals.

I first met 'Tom Hafoty' in the spring of 2002, when he let me watch him work and Peter John shear his sheep. I found the farm, situated high above Llechwedd and nestling just below the brow of the mountain, was a beautiful spot, an ideal place to work, watch and listen to the sounds of pure nature.

The following year he and his wife Blodwen invited me to watch the lambing, a far harder and more difficult event. The pregnant ewe often finds a snug spot sheltered from the elements, which is usually the dry stone walls surrounding the farm. I must admit I missed every actual event but was once lucky enough to watch the ewe pull and lick the birth sack from a new born lamb only a few minutes old.

Back at the farm I managed to sketch a delightful row of young swallows on one of the barn joists and captured Peter shearing and Tom proudly holding just-born twin lambs.

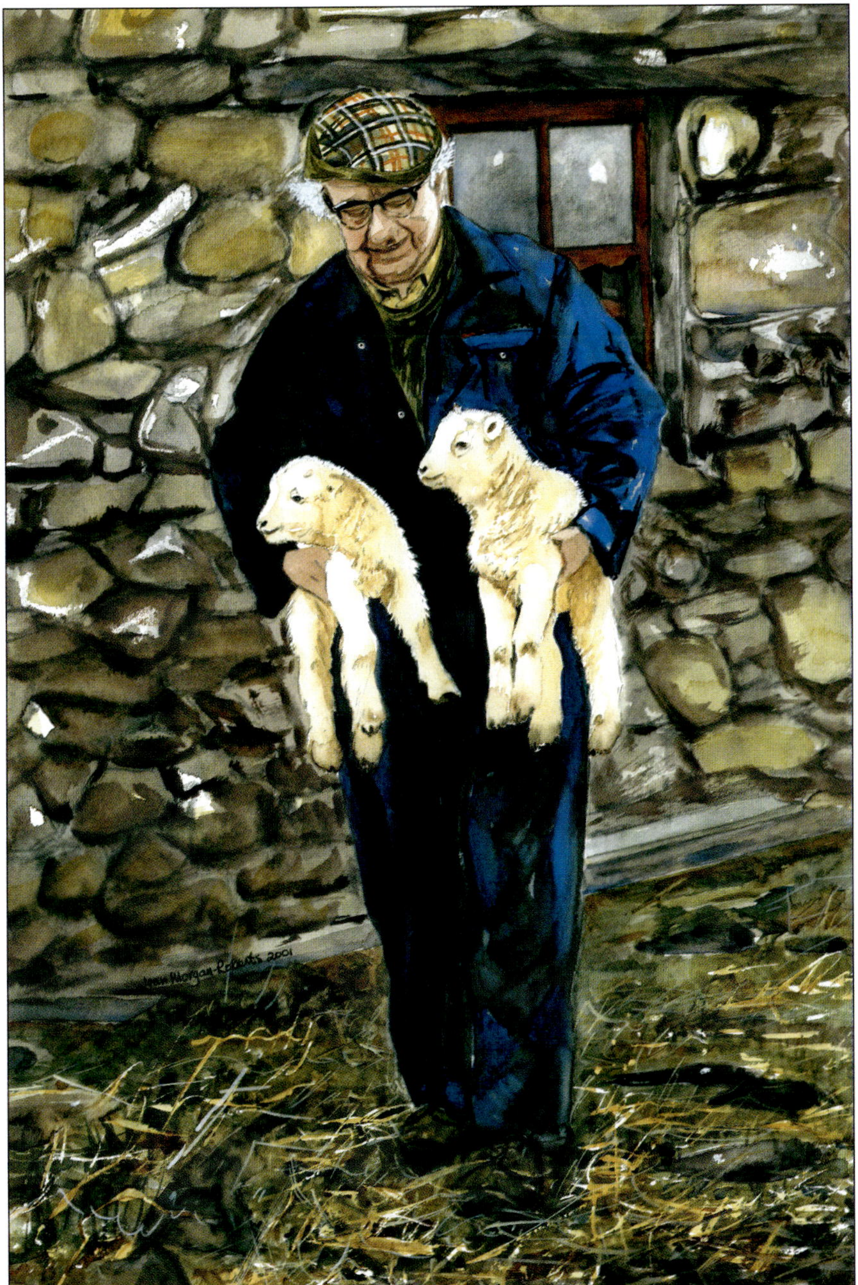
Morgan-Roberts 2001

Hafoty

The family home of David Thomas Jones and his wife Blodwen, this lovely farmhouse is situated above Llechwedd with stunning views of the surrounding hills and valleys.

These newly fledged swallows sat chirping on the upper joist in one of the outhouses on Tom Hafoty's farm. I wonder if they'll be back from Africa next summer and will, like their parents, nest under the eaves.

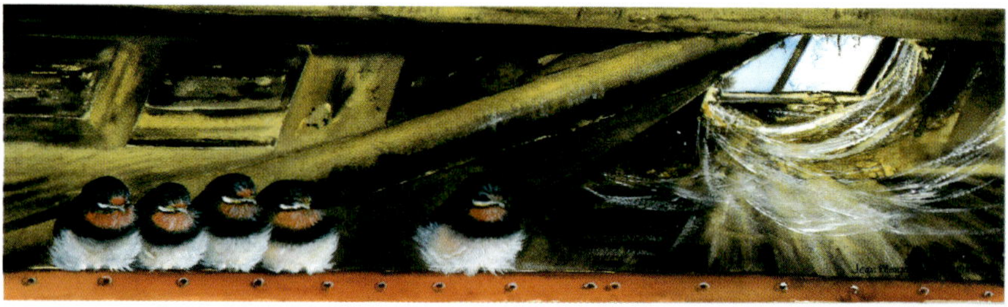

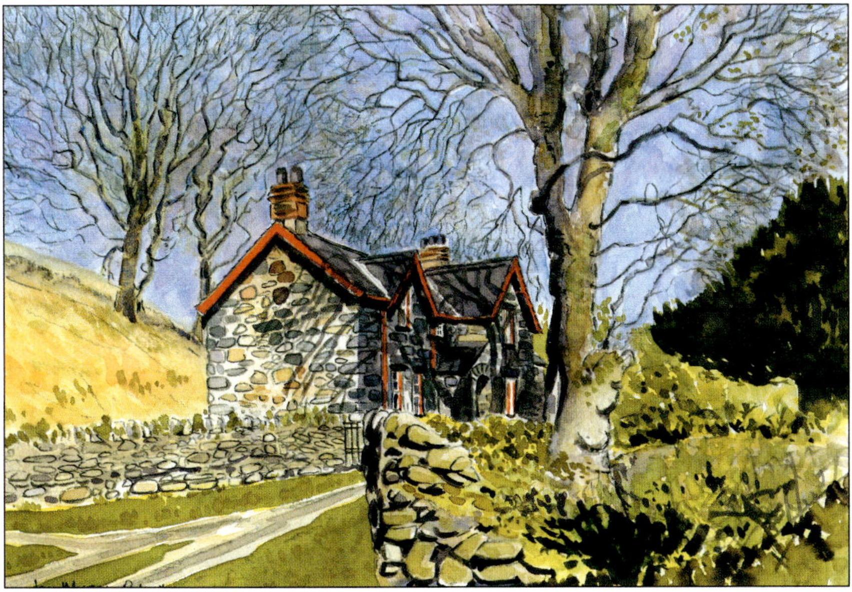

Cymryd

There has probably been a house where beautiful Cymryd stands for many centuries, as the Battle of Cymryd took place hereabouts in around 874 and there are references to 'Kymmeret' in the Bolde Rental of about 1350. It was known as 'Rhodri's revenge' when a Welsh army, under Anarawd totally defeated a Mercian army that had previously killed one of the greatest Welsh kings, Rhodri Mawr. The present building includes a medieval hall house dating from the fifteenth century with its original screen and other timberwork. The solar wing has a date stone 1696 with the initials of Henry and Katherine Lloyd and the motto *Duw a Digon*, but the present owner, Miss Dilys Glynne, has been told that the wing dates from the late sixteenth century, although the staircase and some windows are from 1696. The kitchen is described by the Royal Commission on Ancient and Historical Monuments in Wales and Monmouthshire as 'modern' which probably means eighteenth century. Restoration and improvements were carried out in the 1890s and Miss Glynne added the bathroom extension in 1965. There is a range of outbuildings including a very fine barn, parts of which date probably from around 1835, as dressed stone from Penmaenmawr has been used.

Members of the family, originally Lloyds, have lived here from the sixteenth century, although not continuously, and there are family graves in Gyffin, Caerhun, Llangelynnin and Bangor as well as burial records in Conwy and Dwygyfylchi.

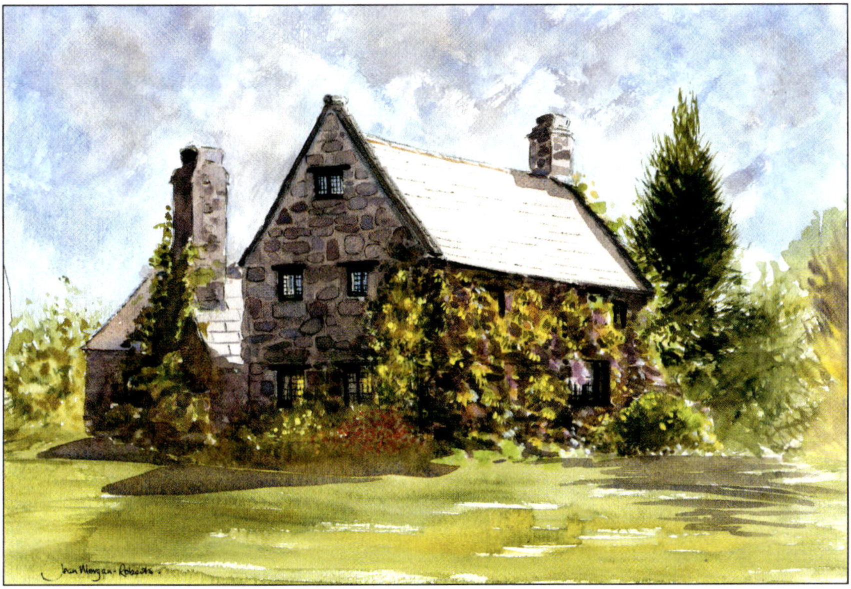

Conwy Castle

King Edward I ordered the castle to be built to defend a foothold for his English occupation forces in Wales. Craftsmen from all over England and the Continent were brought here to work on this masterpiece, hailed as a triumph of military architecture towering on its precipitous rock. The castle's elaborate defences however, betray the weakness of Edward I's position – nowhere else in his captured lands were such protection called for.

The king and his consort Queen Eleanor spent the Christmas of 1283 at the castle. But the castle's triumph proved to be a hollow one – Edward himself was trapped in his own fortress, cut off from his army and provisions during the winter of 1294-5, during the Welsh revolt of Madog ap Llywelyn. The proud king was obliged to live on water and a little honey and even faced the possibility of starvation, until the danger passed.

The castle was easily captured by Owain Glyndŵr during his revolt. During the Wars of the Roses the local Welsh forces made regular raids on Conwy. But when peace returned the castle ceased to be an important stronghold and it was allowed to lay in ruins.

During the Civil War the town's most famous son, John Williams, Archbishop of York, fortified it at his own expense. The castle passed to the Roundheads and held out for three months after the town had fallen. It was dismantled after the Restoration when metal and timber were taken away and shipped to Ireland.

Now it is tourists not warriors who tread the battlements and it is estimated that it attracts around 180,000 visitors a year.

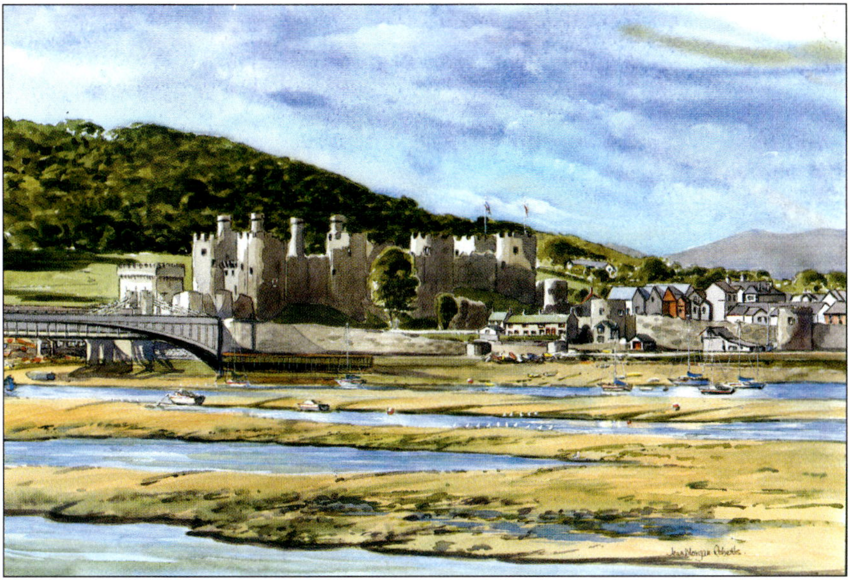

The Black Lion

This gracious house was built by the Vicar of Conwy for his wife and four children in 1589. Over the years it changed use many times, becoming a public house in the 1700s. I grew up in the wonderful old atmosphere of the house with its secret passages, a cellar reputed to have an escape tunnel which led to the quay, a well, stables, stone steps to the town walls, a tower, Elizabethan fireplaces and a beautiful walled garden. To say nothing of the creaky stairs and passageways. I once found half a sovereign under the floorboards of the bedroom over the passageway; this room also had a trap door, probably a means of escape.

The pub lost its licence in the mid 1930s when my father, then a bachelor, bought it to run his electrical business. In the 1950s my mother turned the *Siambr Fawr* – the large chamber – into a tea room where she would delight American visitors with pots of tea and buttered teacakes.

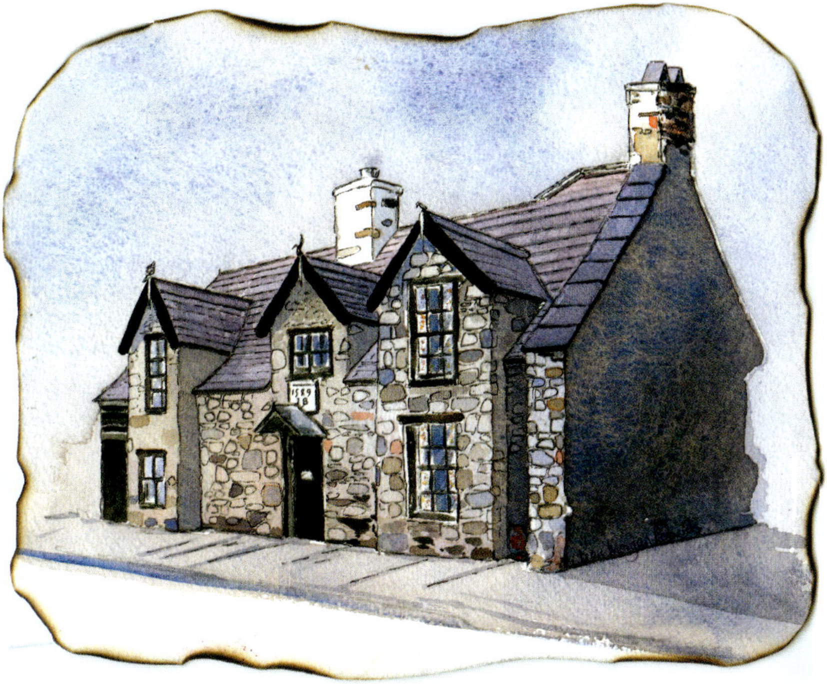

Sir Kyffin Williams RCA

When he was a pupil at the Slade School of Art, Kyffin Williams believed drawing to be a natural ability, a way of swiftly recording something that attracts the eye. He knew what he wanted to paint – people, farmers, landscape and the animals in his own particular part of Wales. Over the years he acquired a knowledge of the world around him, something vitally important to any landscape painter. Many of his drawings were in ink and in watercolour but most were in pencil in small notebooks, the easiest way to work when the elements are at their worst, he maintained.

Born on Anglesey in 1918 he went to Shrewsbury School where he won an art prize and in 1941 was declared to be unfit by the army doctor and refused admission to the Royal Welch Fusiliers on medical grounds and advised to take up art as therapy. After many years of teaching, travelling and painting he returned to Wales in 1974, was the first Welsh member elected to the Royal Cambrian Academy whose headquarters is at Conwy and became its president.

For the last 33 years he lived in an old cottage on his native island. Once a tavern and before that the home of a Bristol slave ship captain, it is in an idyllic setting at the side of a tiny cove on the shores of the Menai Strait with a panoramic view of Snowdonia.

He applied to the Winston Churchill Memorial Trust to visit Patagonia, under the somewhat false premise that he could ride the 400 miles across the pyth prairie from Trelew to Cwm Hyfryd. When Kyffin died in September 2006, he was hailed the greatest artist of his century in Wales and the person who had done more than anyone else to promote and popularise art in this country.

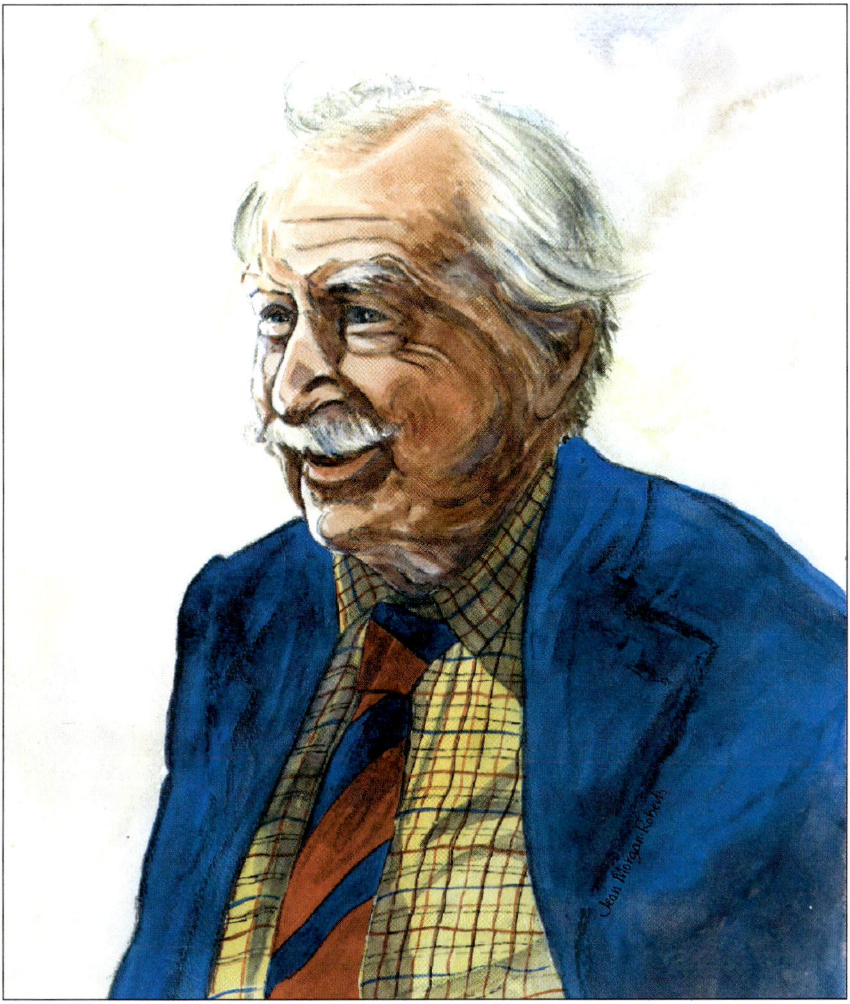

Peggy Rowlands

One of the most striking figures Conwy has known in recent years was undoubtedly Peggy Rowlands. Tall and stately in her colourful clothes and never without a big hat, Peggy lived in the last house in the lower end of High Street leading to the quay and here she tended a tiny garden she had cultivated at the back and watered the profusion of colourful plants in her yard, stopping to have a word with nearly everyone who went by.

Such were Peggy's looks and deportment that those who did not know her speculated wildly on who she was. Some said she had been an actress, others thought her a model but Peggy had been neither. She was born into one of the oldest families in the town, the Hugheses, who have been fishing in the river for more than 500 years and married Tommy Rowlands, a scrap metal dealer whose family had lived in the house at the bottom of High Street for many generations.

People were drawn to Peggy. She radiated beauty and grace but apart from these attributes she had a deep understanding of humanity. She listened to tales of happiness and of woe, she kept confidences and offered words of comfort. And she knew everyone, from local residents to regular holidaymakers who used to seek her out every year, and one of her redeeming features was that she never ran anyone down, always finding something good to say. And visitors were fascinated by her collection of dolls displayed in her front window.

The town was stunned by her death. It was difficult to imagine walking down to the harbour and not seeing her in one of her many flamboyant outfits, always beautifully colour co-ordinated, against a background of the plants she so lovingly cultivated.

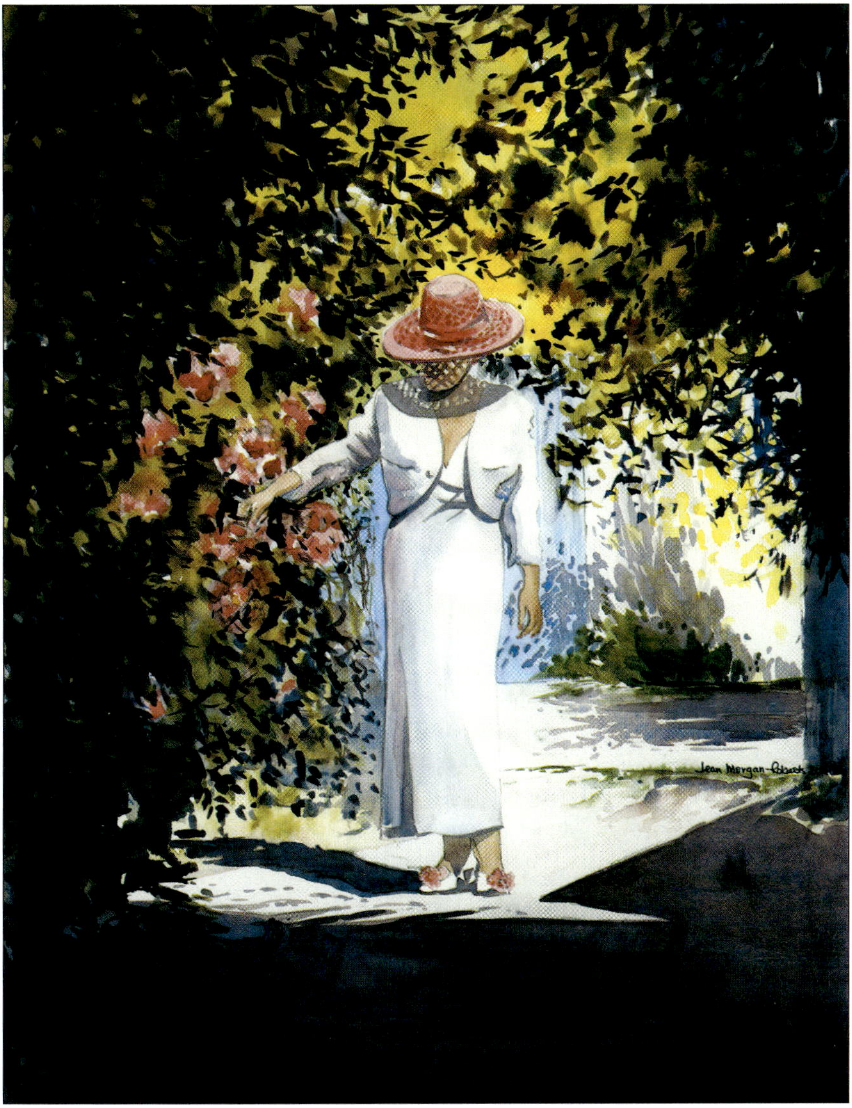
Jean Morgan-Black

Margaret Williams

Journalist, broadcaster and lecturer Margaret Williams returned to the land of her fathers after 20 years spent working on newspapers when she took over the Smallest House in Britain from her mother, Elizabeth.

The house has been owned by her family for many generations and the last tenant was a fisherman who was six feet three inches tall. In 1900 the house, along with other cottages which were slightly bigger, was condemned for human habitation and the then editor of the *North Wales Weekly News*, Mr J. Roger Dawson, persuaded her great grandfather, Robert Jones, to tour the country measuring small houses to prove that his was the tiniest of the lot. This he did, and the house was opened to the public and eventually it was included in *The Guinness Book of Records.*

Over the years the house became one of Conwy's top attractions. Visitors come from all over the world to marvel at the minute interior, a cosy sitting room furnished in Victorian style and a narrow bedroom. There is a commentary in 22 languages and Margaret has written three books about it – *The Smallest House in Great Britain, A Man Called Jones and his Smallest House* and *The Smallest House Cook Book.* She has also written *The Sea Sous at the Smallest House* which is one of a series of books telling the history of Conwy to children.

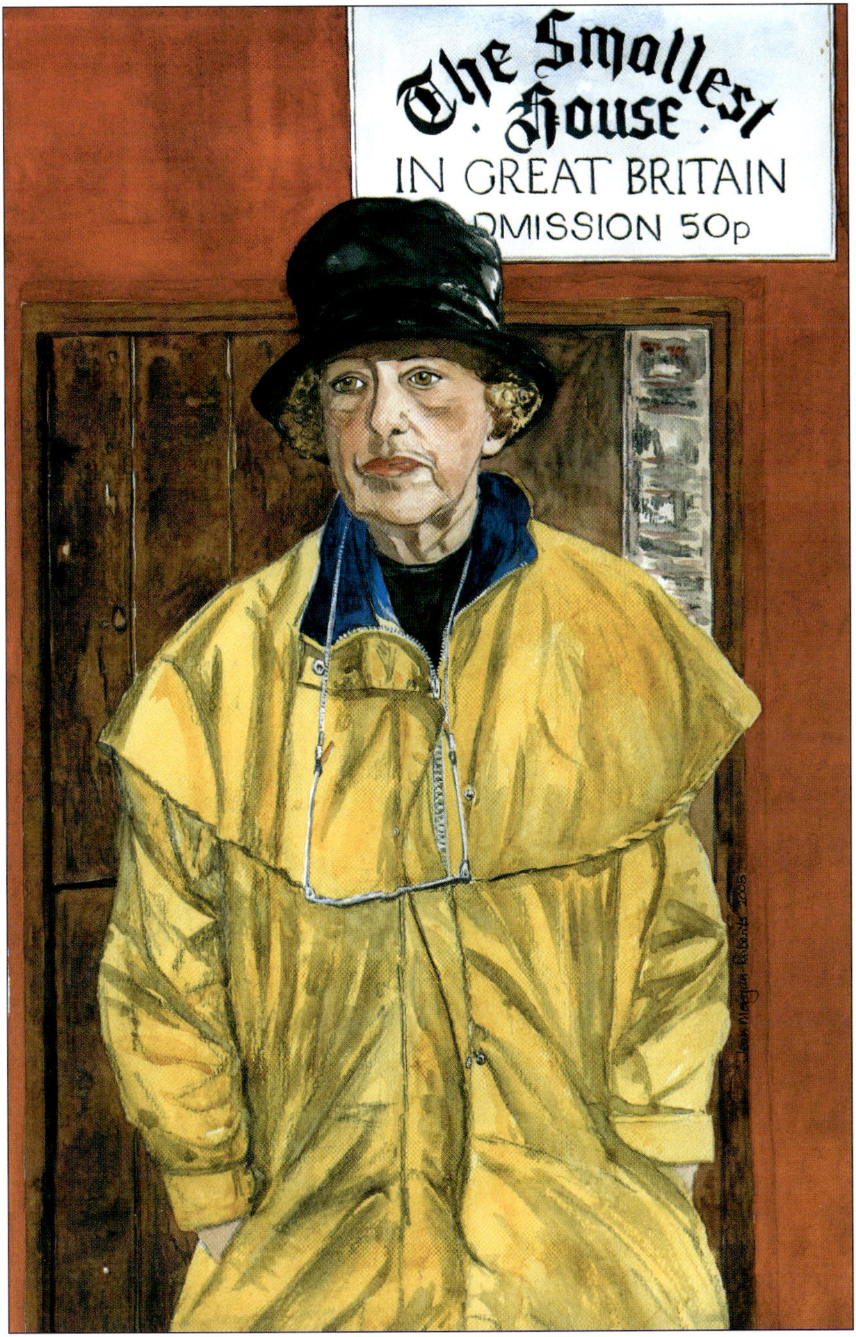
The Smallest House
IN GREAT BRITAIN
DMISSION 50p

Dr Michael Senior

Born in Llandudno, Michael has, since 1950, lived at Bryn Eisteddfod, Glan Conwy, famous for its historic garden which is open to the public on the last Sunday in May every year.

Michael holds a doctorate in philosophy and is a full-time writer with more than 30 books published. Many of these are on the subject of local history, such as *Portrait of North Wales; The Crossing of the Conwy;* and others on Anglesey, Snowdonia, Meirionnydd, the Conwy Valley and the Llŷn peninsular. Some, such as *North Wales in the Making, The Standing Stones of North-western Wales, Hillforts of northern Wales,* and *Cromlechs and Cairns,* deal with the geology and early history of the area. Some delve into mythology and others investigate historical mysteries such as *Llys Helyg* and *The Myths of the Lost Lands, Did Prince Madog discover America?* and *Did Lewis Carroll visit Llandudno?*

When not writing he is deeply involved with conservation issues and has been secretary of the Conwy Civic Society for the past 40 years. He also travels extensively, in Africa, the Far East and the Americas and has a particular fondness for Greece, about which he has written a book, *Greece and its Myths.*

Michael is also a part-time painter, having had a number of works exhibited at the Royal Cambrian Academy where he is chairman of the Friends and has been appointed an Honorary Academician.

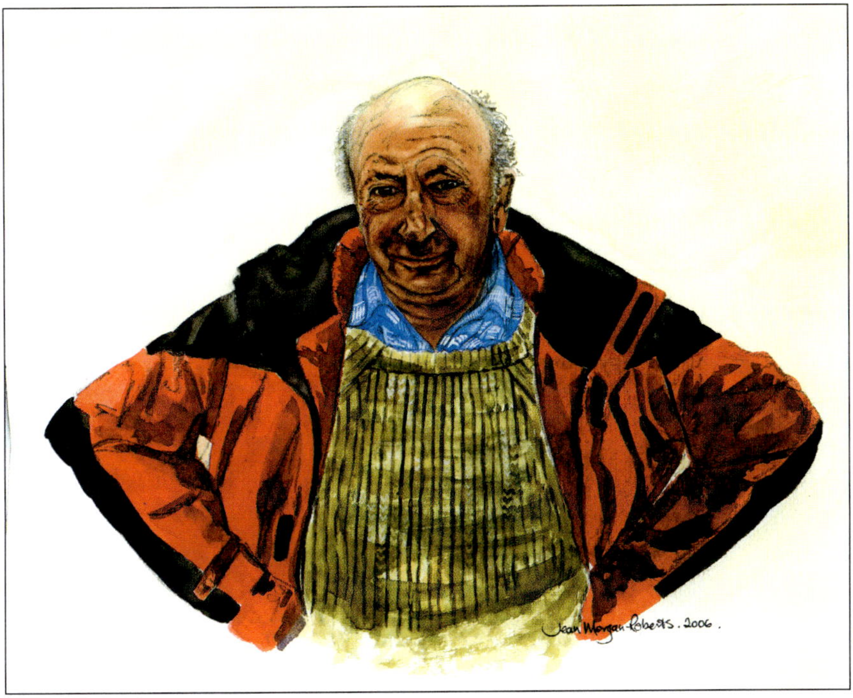
Jean Morgan-Roberts. 2006.

Keith Robinson
Butcher and pigeon fancier

In the days when Conwy was a busy market town Keith and his father were familiar figures behind the counter at their butcher's shop in High Street. At that pre-supermarket time this was one of five butchers' shops, while there were eight grocers as well as fishmongers and greengrocers, and like many other traders, Keith lived above the shop when he married his wife Diane.

The Robinson family moved from Bramhall in Cheshire to Conwy in 1947 when Keith was seven years old and he soon became part of the young local community. When he was 14 he began his love affair with racing pigeons, which continues to this day.

Since he joined the Llandudno Saturday Homing Society 50 years ago he has released his pigeons every Saturday from April to September. He feels he has grown up with his birds, first by training them to fly back from short local distances like Flint, Mold and Wrexham. In those days he would put the pigeons on a train and when they reached their destination the station master would release them for the journey home. Now, they travel by a special transporter which starts at Deganwy and picks up at various points along the coast.

'Like any athlete they need to build themselves up for the long distance race home,' said Keith, whose best pigeon won the Bonn (Germany) to Conwy race two years running.

Keith is now the oldest member of the Llandudno club, has 60 pigeons and has always been interested in wild life.

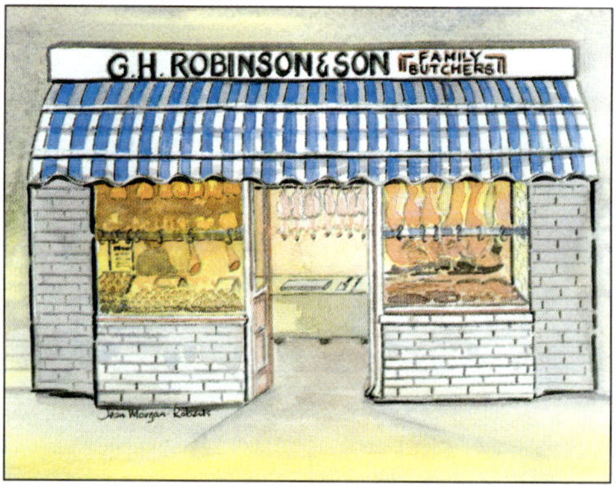

G. H. Robinson & Son Family Butchers, High Street, Conwy 1960s. When food I'm sure tasted more like the 'real' thing!

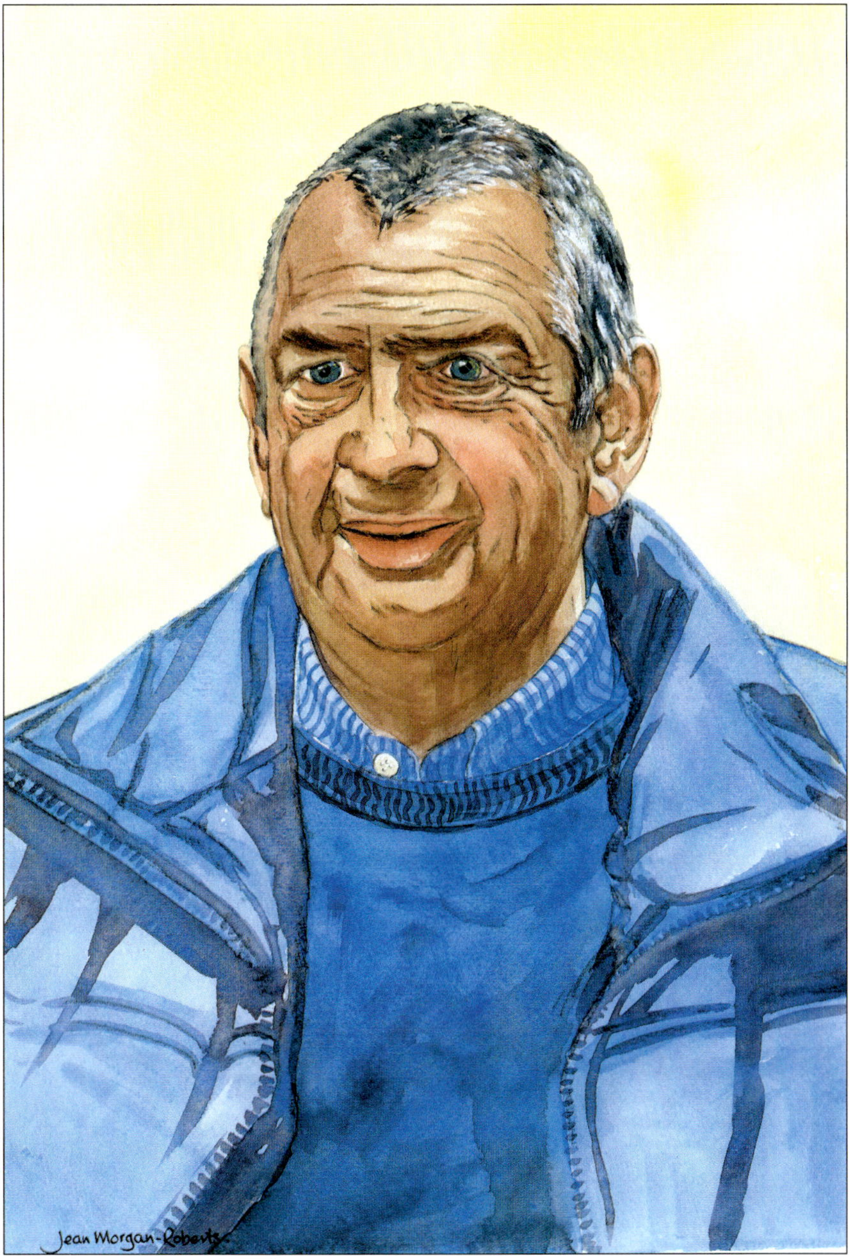
Jean Morgan-Roberts

Ivor Peris Roberts

When Ivor was growing up he was a familiar figure in Conwy in his bright yellow oilskin and sou'westr – in all weathers! He had acquired the outfit because, delivering milk to most of the houses and shops in the town, he was soaked to the skin and one particularly miserable morning his boss, Mr Richards, took him to J. P. Griffiths, the men's outfitters in Castle Street where he was rigged out to cope with the elements. But he was so pleased with the yellow gear he wore it even when the sun was shining!

Leaving school at 14, he became an apprentice gardener for Mrs Craven at the Old Rectory, Gyffin. He enjoyed the work but dreaded having to take her pekingese 'Ting-y-Ling' for a walk, and being heard calling him to heel, running to the woods and hiding lest his friends see him.

When he was 18 he wanted to join the Royal Navy and his father said he would put him down for 20 years, but he never made it. He served with the South Wales Borderers in East Africa and on returning home worked at the Dolgarrog Aluminium works and was later at the Hotpoint factory.

He retired in 1998 but his wife Jean Morgan-Roberts opened her gallery that year and he became househusband. She states she could never have kept the gallery open or found time to paint without his dedication to their home. 'He's a star,' she says.

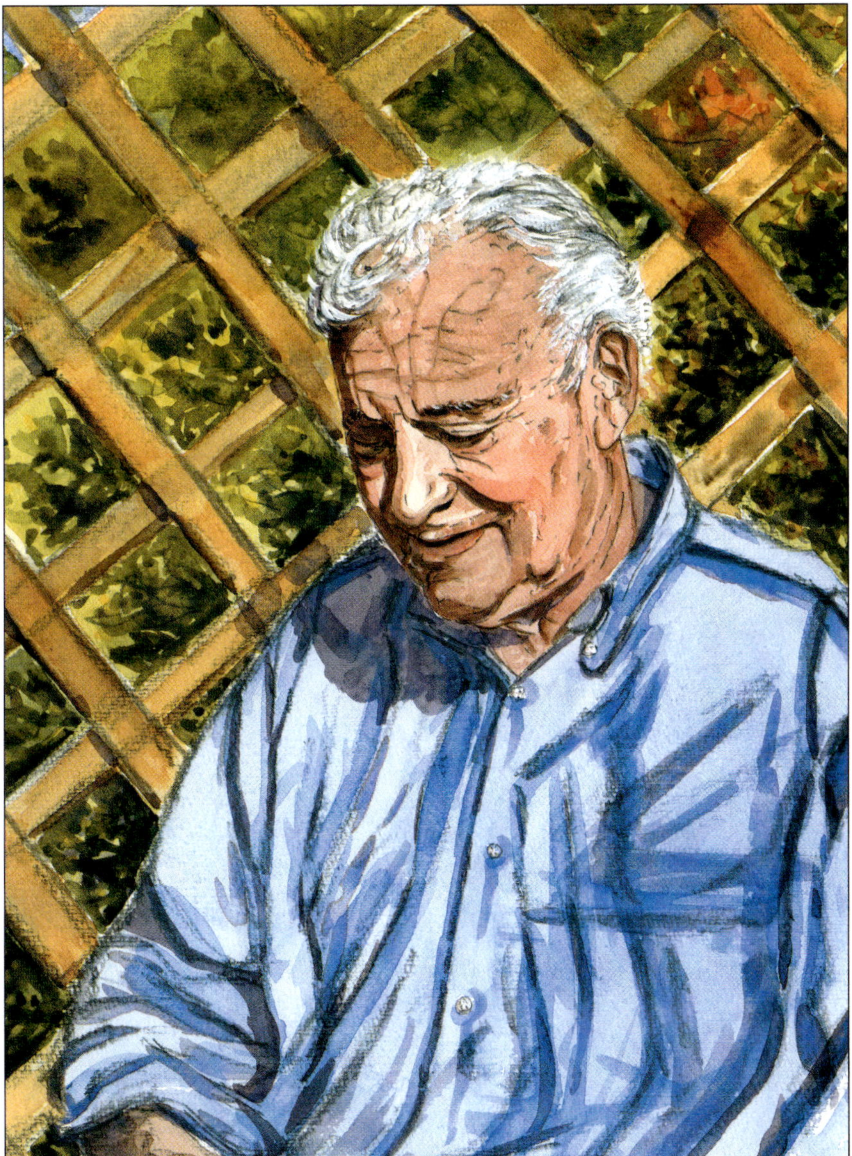

Hugh Roberts

Hugh Roberts reckons he was fortunate to be born in Rhosllannerchrugog which was then the largest village in Wales, famous for its choirs and a poet and a couple of titled people and at one time he lived in the house of Welsh hymn writer Dr Caradoc Roberts.

Leaving school at 14, Hugh worked as an apprentice hairdresser for seven shillings and sixpence a week, and then went on to Astons furniture factory for more money. Part of his national service in the RAF was spent in Germany where he was involved in the Berlin Airlift. Later he worked with the county fire service in Wrexham and was awarded the Bronze Medal of the RSPCA for rescuing a sheepdog trapped 100 feet down a mine shaft. In 1970 he was promoted and transferred to Colwyn Bay and on retirement was sports centre manager at Llandrillo College.

He has served two terms as Town Mayor of Conwy, is a school governor and a member of the international association of Lions Clubs and belongs to two choirs, the Maelgwn Male Voice Choir and Côr Cymysg Dyffryn Conwy. And in his younger days he was a racing cyclist, winning medals for his efforts.

He and his wife Betty are keen workers for charity, and were once on a rota driving elderly people to weekly meetings.

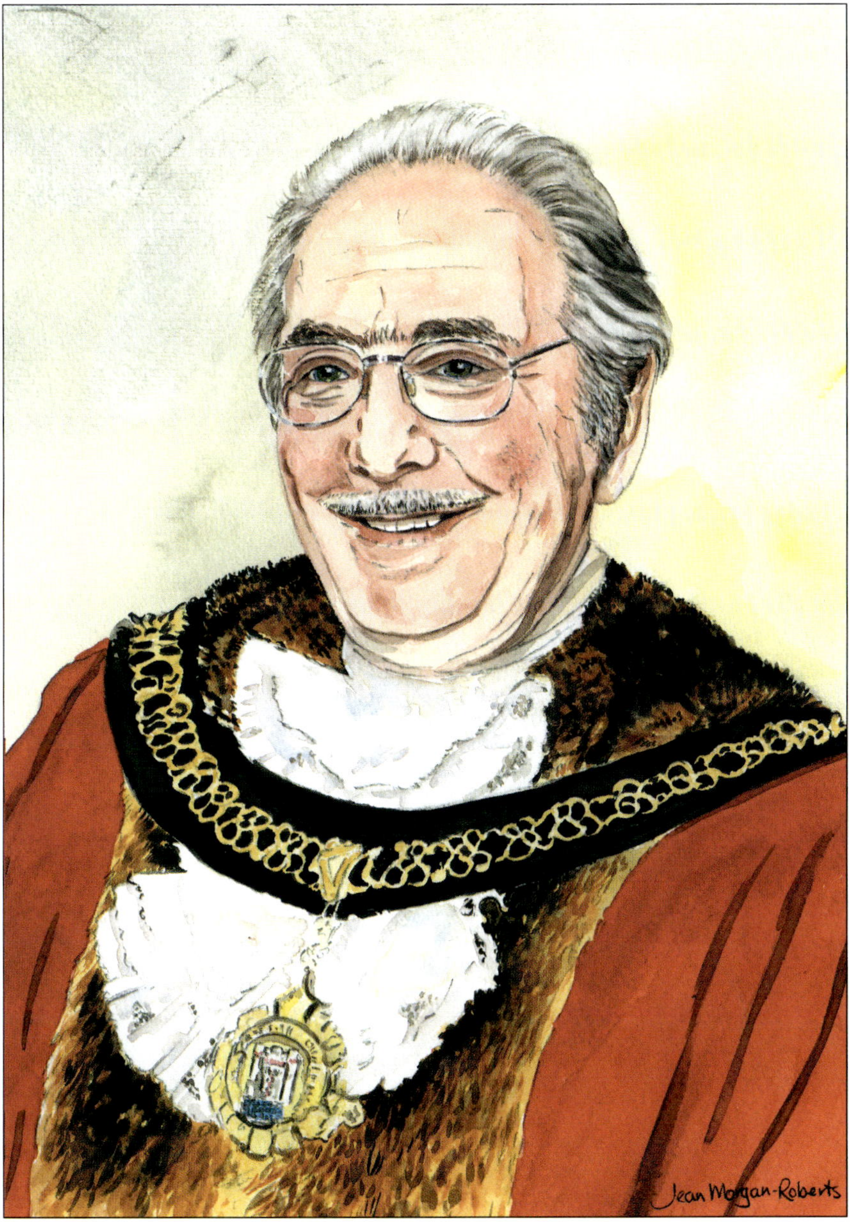
Jean Morgan-Roberts

Betty Pattinson, OBE

Elizabeth Mair (Betty) Pattinson is one of Conwy's Jackdaws, the name given to those born within the town walls, these days an exclusive breed as most babies first see the light of day in maternity hospitals. Her father, William Owen Roberts and her mother, Gwen were descendants of three of the oldest fishing and lifeboat families in the area – Roberts, Jones and Owen.

Betty has given exceptional service to her native town. She was Mayor of Conwy and Constable of the castle in 1976-77 and 1989-90, and Mayor of Aberconwy Borough Council in 1986-87. In 1986 she was made OBE for services to local government and the local community. She is a well-known local historian, having produced two books on Conwy and its characters and events, is past president of Aberconwy Historical Society.

She has also been a member of the Court of Governors of the National Museum of Wales and of its Council, the Court of Governors of the University of Wales and many other national and local bodies and charities.

Betty is married to Mitchell Pattinson, former chief public health officer of Colwyn Bay and their large family live nearby.

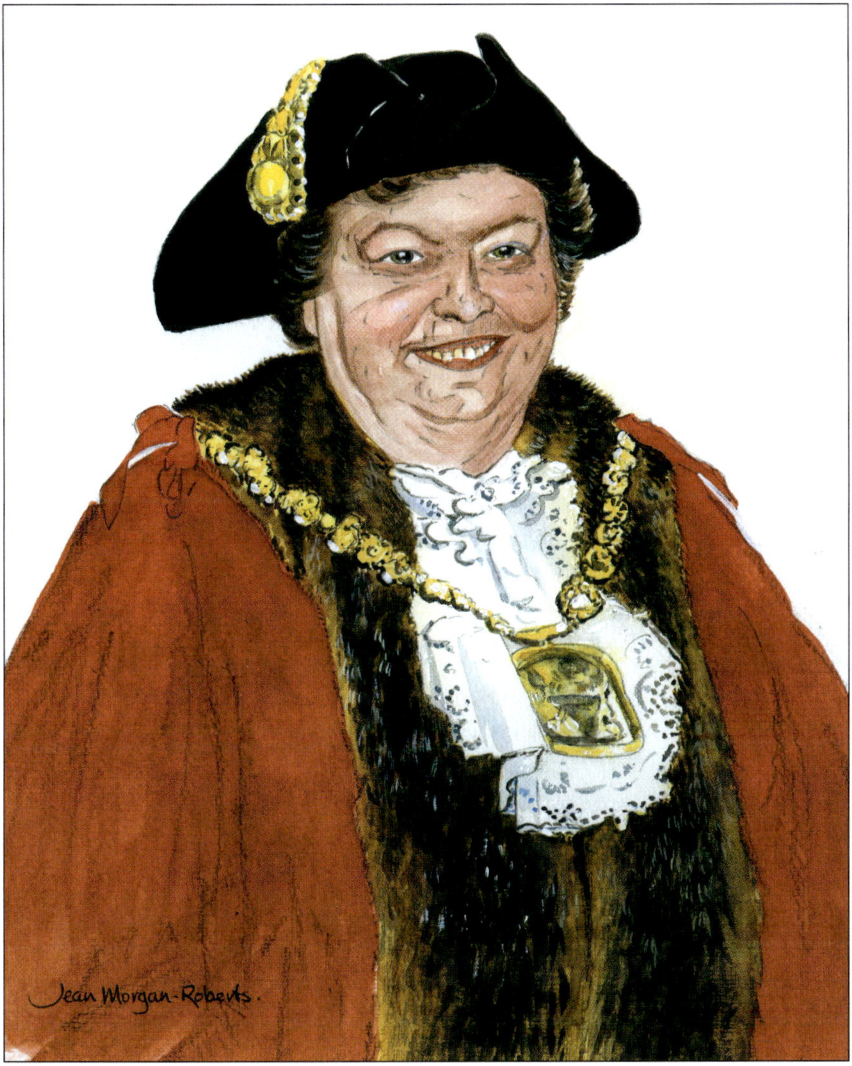
Jean Morgan-Roberts.

David Gwynfor Price

Greeting the countless visitors that flock to Conwy, David Gwynfor Price is following an ancient tradition that goes back to 1066 when news that William of Normandy was invading Britain was passed from town to town by men specially chosen to announce the king's messages.

The only voluntary town crier in northern Wales, David can be seen every Tuesday welcoming tourists who alight from coaches in the main car park and informing them of the many attractions Conwy has to offer, and as soon as he appears in his flamboyant costume and tricorn hat cameras start to click and his picture has gone to many parts of the world.

But it is not only his picture that has travelled the globe. He has taken part in town crying contests in the United States, Canada and Germany as well as in many parts of this country and he has a wealth of stories about his exploits.

When he went to a competition on the Isle of Wight he visited a waxworks exhibition and in the Chamber of Horrors two women thought he was one of the exhibits and prodded him with an umbrella, only to scream when he winked at them and spoke.

One of his proudest moments was when he met Diana, Princess of Wales at a charity event and she expressed a great interest in what he did.

But being a well-known face can result in embarrassing experiences. Like the time he was chased by a group of girls on Rhyl promenade. They were screaming for his autograph but had mistaken him for Pavarotti.

Throughout the summer his deep baritone voice is as familiar as the cries of the seagulls as he makes his many proclamations throughout the day.

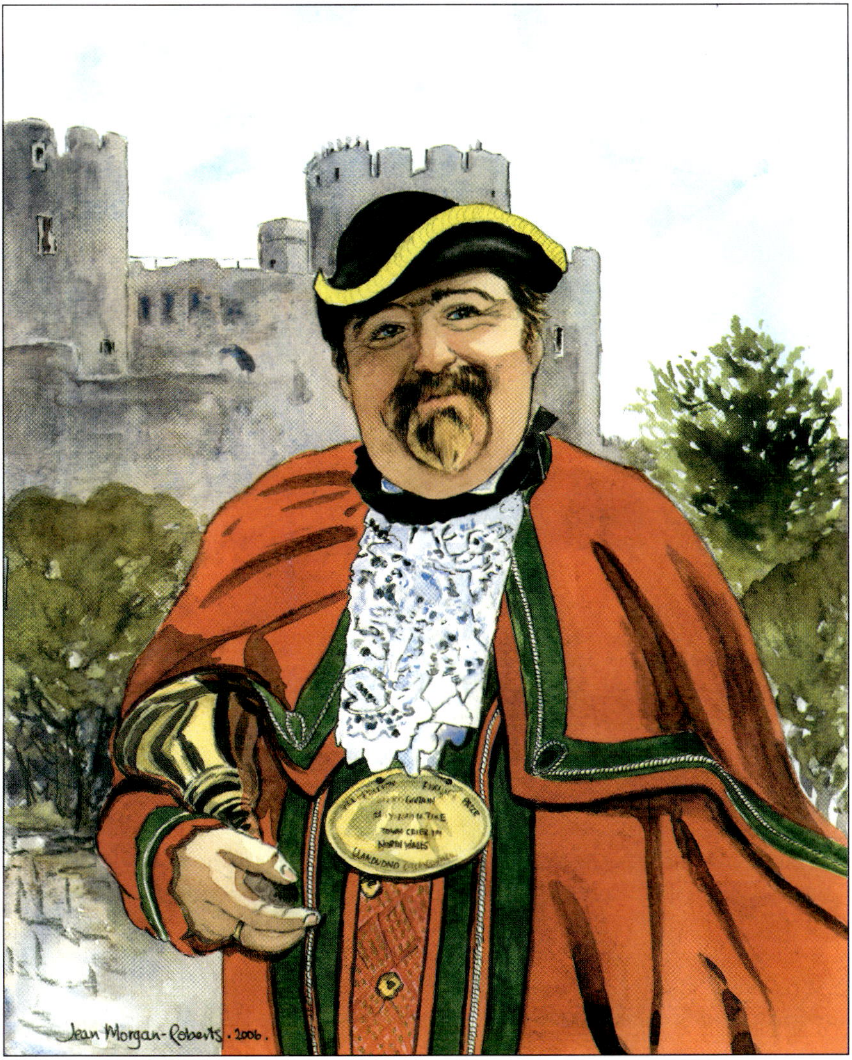
PRIZE
TOWN CRIER IN
NORTH WALES
LLANDUDNO
Jean Morgan-Roberts. 2006.

Peter McFadden

When Peter McFadden came to live in north Wales in 1973 he little thought he would be the one who would revive the Conwy fairs.

Then a production engineer at Hotpoint, Peter went to have a look at the Honey Fair which was a sad spectacle, having been moved from Castle Street and High Street to the Vicarage car park in order to reduce traffic congestion. He expected to see lots of beekeepers selling their products, but there was only one honey stall.

Peter bought a jar of honey and became interested in bees. He joined the new Aberconwy Beekeepers' Association and bought two hives of bees. Soon he had a stall at the fair and now it has returned to High Street he is there every year, standing outside the Pen-y-Bryn tearoom.

In 1990 he became secretary of the Beekeepers' Association. 'We had a lovely summer that year and our best ever honey harvest,' he said. 'My bees produced 1,600 pounds of honey from 20 hives. I realised that the beekeepers had to start organising the Honey Fair or it would die. I publicised it widely, a newspaper ran a feature on it and this brought in plenty of stalls and visitors. In 1992 the Conwy tunnel was opened and this meant visitors could enjoy seeing the town without the heavy traffic.

'The fair has continued to grow every year and it is now a major event and stall space is still free of charge. I'm still obsessed with beekeeping after nearly 30 years. In 2005 I sold 340 jars at the Honey Fair.'

Peter also organises the Seed Fair every March. This has also become a major event with many local nurseries offering unusual plants.

These two fairs are rooted in history and are as old as the town itself. When Edward I of England conquered Wales he decreed that the Welsh people were not to live in the new town he had built here at Conwy. In order to help them remain solvent he allowed them to trade within the walls on one day each week, but they had to leave at sunset. Over the years this concession led to fairs being held in the street, and at the beginning of the twentieth century nine of them were held each year. These dwindled to two, the Honey Fair and the Seed Fair.

Peter floated the idea of a Conwy food festival which was an immediate success and he is responsible for the Village Gardens open day at Ro-wen, where he lives, which raises funds for the local Memorial Hall.

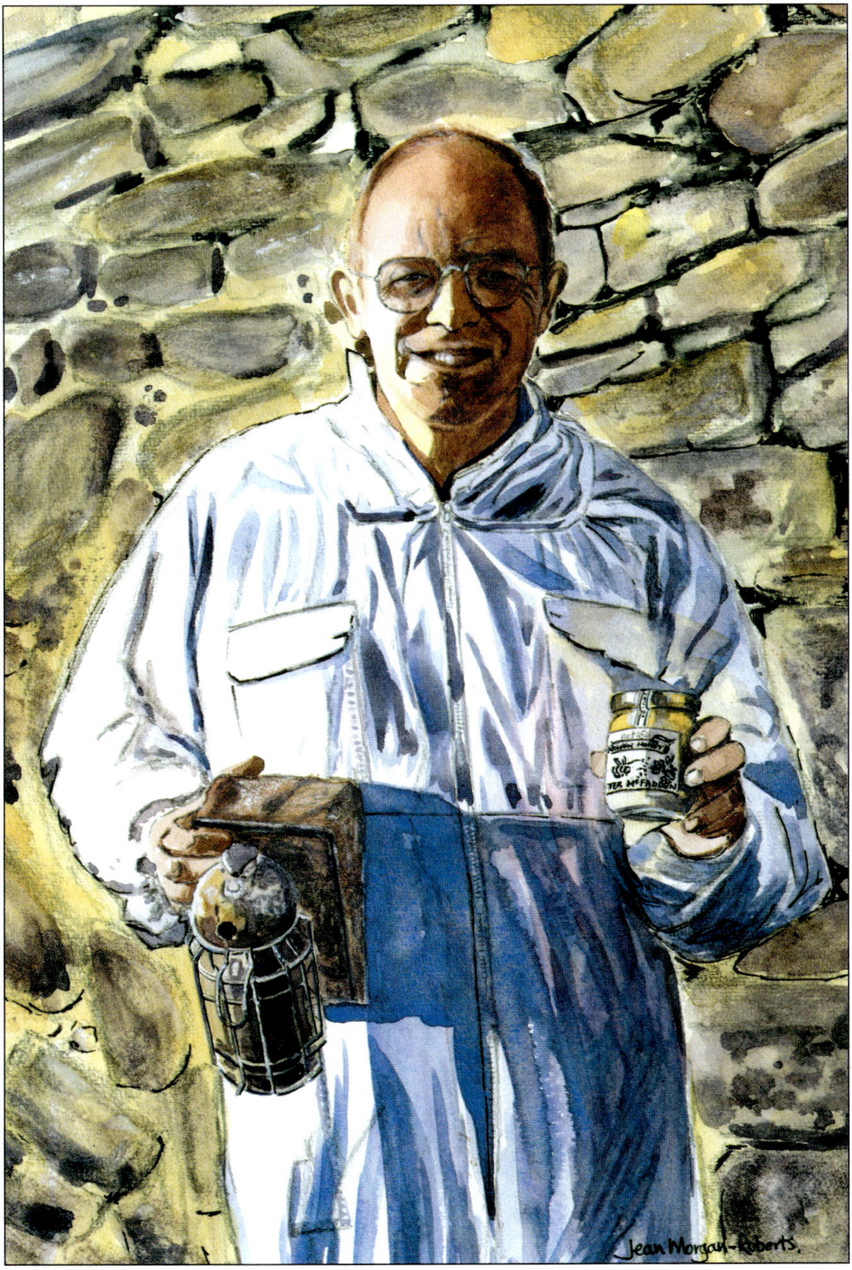
Jean Morgan-Roberts.

Tom Morris

Tom Morris, at 90, still tends the hens and sheep at his hill farm above Glan Conwy with its sweeping views over the valley and the slow meandering river.

He has spent all his nine decades in the Welsh mountains; he was raised on his parents' farm near Abergele when horses drew ploughs and cows were hand-milked. Later he moved to Garnedd Wen, a smallholding 1,000 feet above Conwy with a matchless vista of the distant town and its spectacular castle. From Garnedd Wen he ran a riding centre, leading a string of sturdy mountain ponies on treks over the hills. His own horse was a chestnut Arab called Herod that once served time as polo pony and could turn on a sixpence. Tom, tall and ramrod straight in the saddle, was a superb horseman.

Tom was also keeper of the key to Llangelynnin old church, which he still visits for the Harvest Festival. There his remarkable baritone voice, which earned him lead roles in Colwyn Bay Operatic Society productions as a young man, still fills the little church. He could have made a career in singing – instead he chose to remain a farmer, in the hills that have always been his home.

He now lives on a less remote farm, closer to village and shops, and can still be seen walking the fields at lambing time with his sheepdogs Jack and Jill. Having no intention of retiring, he finds age has not curtailed his plans and he has just built a vast new house for his hens.

Tom cannot imagine a life beyond the wild expanses of his native Snowdonia, neither could he envisage a world without his beloved animals.

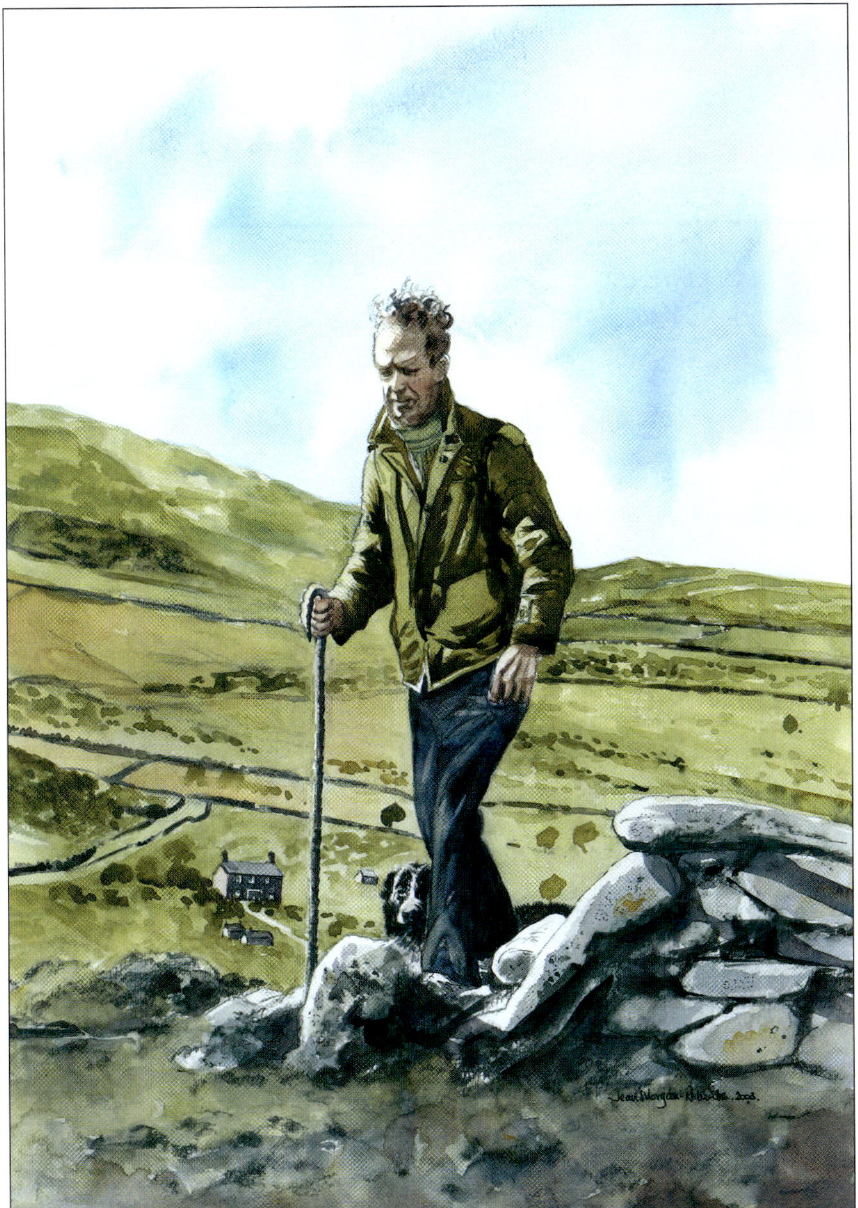

Doctor Geoff Moore

Although he went to school and worked outside Wales, in Manchester and Liverpool, family links with northern Wales have been magnetic throughout Dr Geoff Moore's life. In the early 1950s his father owned a house near Betws-y-coed which at the time was surrounded by an absorbing wilderness and when this was sold its absence could not be satisfied, even by a large suburban garden.

In the early 1970s the combination of restricted expensive oil supplies and the miners' strike produced the three-day week, which meant that where he was living there were long power cuts and water shortages and this became the incentive to find a place with the possibility of a more self-sufficient lifestyle. Naturally, northern Wales and particularly the Conwy valley was the place to look.

After two years of searching and many disappointments he and his wife Kathleen found a small house by a stream with its own water supply and a history of domestic electricity generating which was ideal for a growing family.

Their first product was honey. Kathleen became one of the original members of the Aberconwy Beekeepers' Association and the first to win the Berry Memorial Shield, awarded for a range of bee products. In the early 1980s they were able to buy extra land, becoming less horticultural and more agricultural. They had goats for milk and sheep for wool and meat.

In the early days they had valued help from neighbours with their sheep. This led them to appreciate that caring for sheep, on and off the mountain, has always required communal co-operation and still does.

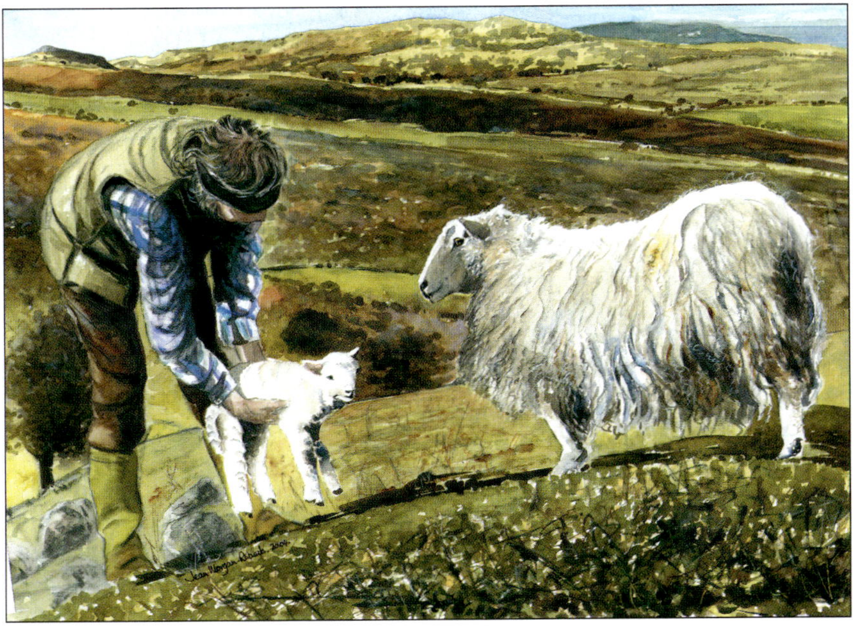

Peter Hugh John

Born in Groesffordd, Peter Hugh John has lived with his younger brother Peris Richard in the same house for 48 years.

Peter Hugh farms a small area of land near his home at Hendre where he keeps around 60 sheep. In mid-September, after the flock has lambed, he takes them to Llanrwst, Ruthin or St Asaph, the nearest of the few remaining markets in the area.

His busiest time is in June and July, when he is much needed by the local farming community to help shear hundreds of sheep. But he is busy throughout the year repairing or rebuilding dry stone walling.

Peter has only left the Conwy valley once – for a week on the Isle of Man. He has no intention of going away again – he is happy looking after his neighbours in this little corner of Wales he calls his own.

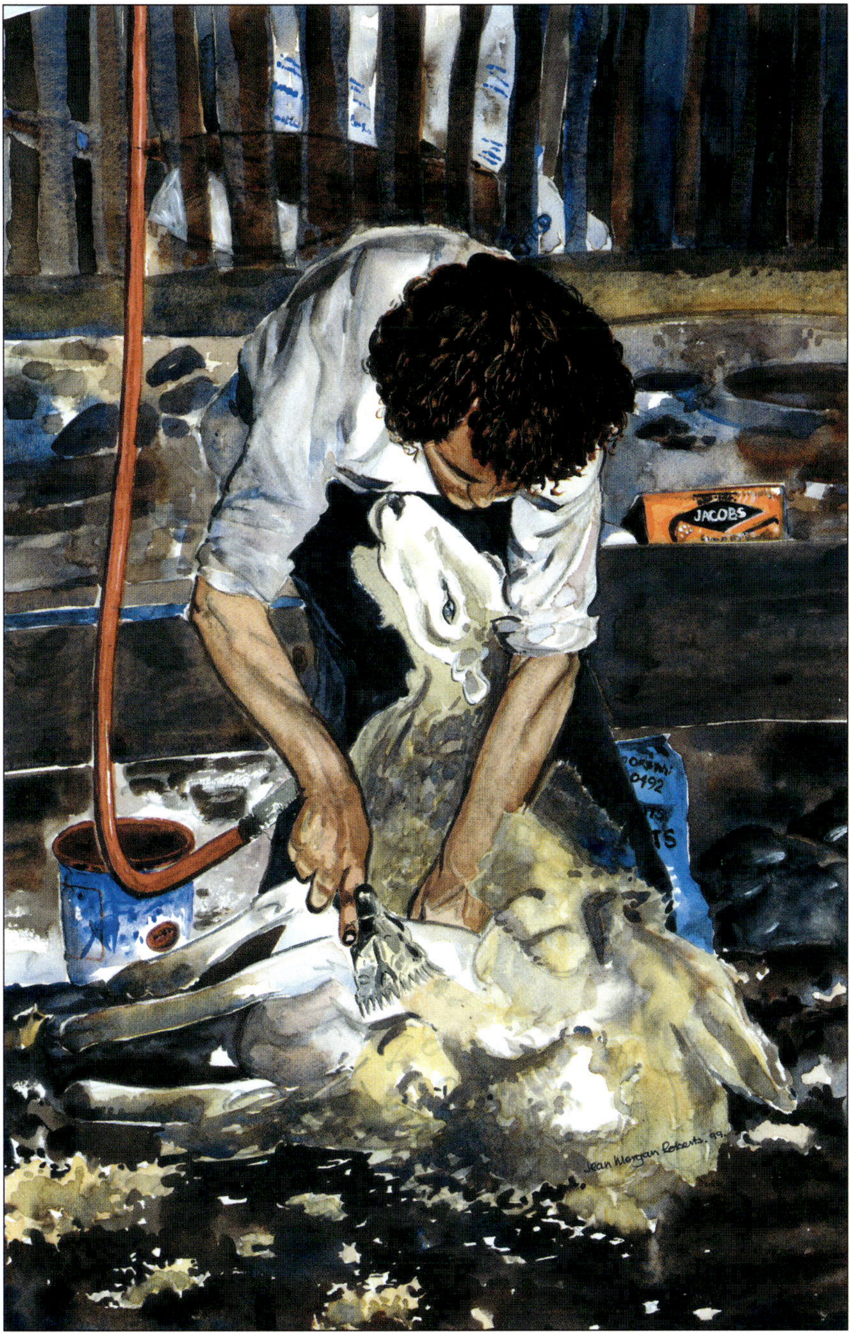
JACOBS
Jean Morgan Roberts. 99.

Raymond Hughes

The son of one of Conwy's most colourful characters, Sion Hughes, Raymond inherited his father's business and great chunks of his personality as well.

His first job was that of tea boy at the building of the Mulberry Harbour, a closely guarded secret operation on the Morfa that played a vital part in the Allied invasion of Europe.

When hostilities ended he helped his father and eventually took over the business himself.

Soon he was selling his wares at the Conwy weekly market and then he branched out, visiting every fair and market in north Wales. He sold everything from massive carpets to tiny ornaments, travelling along the coast and into the surrounding countryside with his heavily laden lorry containing all manner of treasures.

Few outside events were held without Raymond and his wide selection of goods being present and regular market-goers came to rely on him when they were searching for something special or unusual.

His stall was one of the highlights of the Honey Fair held in Conwy in September and the Seed Fair in March where he delighted customers with his witty repartee.

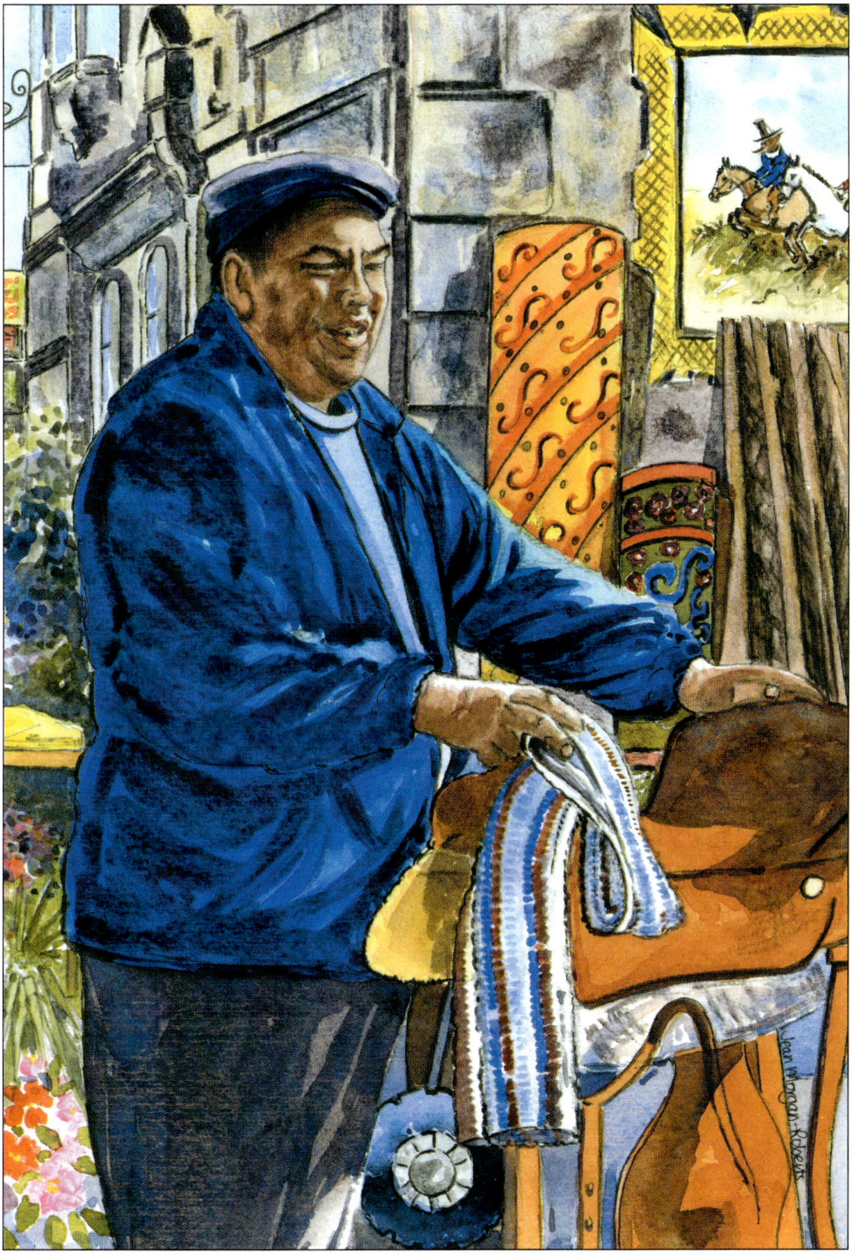
Jean Morgan-Roberts

Ken Rimmer Hughes

Conwy's oldest fisherman, Ken Rimmer Hughes, has spent all his life in Berry Street, in the shadow of the town walls. He and his wife Denise, who was also born in the same street to an old local family, are the only husband and wife members of the Conwy Jackdaw Society, an exclusive organisation open only to those born within the town walls.

Ken is from a long line of seafarers. His grandfather came to Conwy from Blackpool and he and his sons were part of the mussel fleet which Ken joined when he left school at the age of 14, having worked during holidays and at weekends for some years before that, going out to the estuary in all weathers with a 20-foot long rake.

Not that all his life has been spent mussel gathering. He was a crew man on two of the Conwy-based trawlers for a time, the *Penorva* and the *Glen Maye* and while he enjoyed the experience he found he preferred musselling because it allowed him to spend more time at home.

'Mussel fishing is seasonal, from September to April, so before it starts we spend the time getting the purification tanks ready,' he says. 'We cannot sell mussels unless they are purified.'

During the war Ken worked on the Mulberry Harbour, the structures used in the D-Day landings during World War II. He and another fisherman, Sam Craven, ferried equipment from the Deganwy dock across the river. 'We didn't know what was happening – nobody around here did,' he said of this highly secret operation. 'You would never believe they towed it all the way to France.'

'They built two different slipways at Conwy. One was like a big concrete block and another looked like the rigs with big iron work. There is a plaque at the harbour commemorating Conwy's contribution.'

His friend Raymond Hughes was a tea boy on the site and years later when a pub opened there and was appropriately called The Mulberry, they were both asked to pull the first pint!

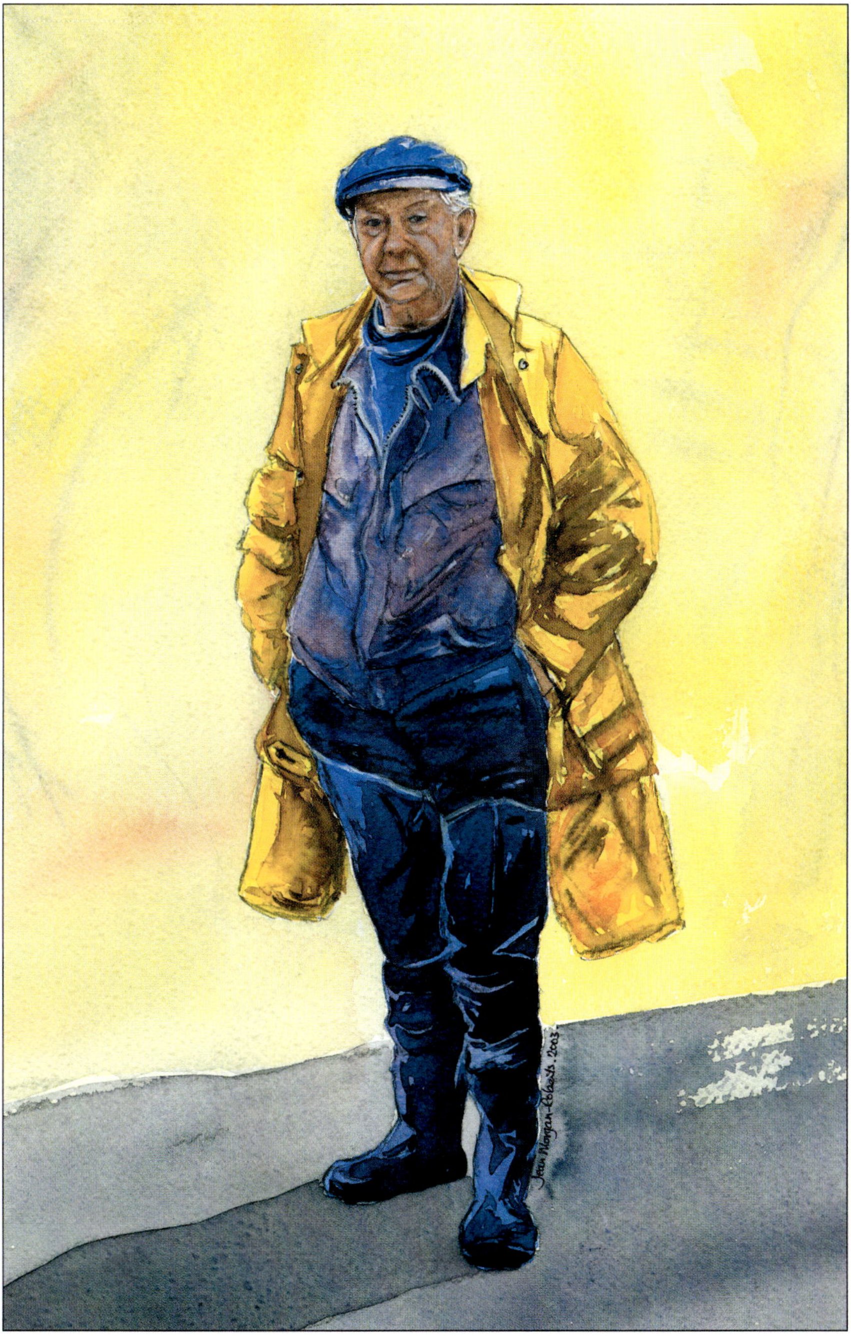

Bryn Hughes

The voice of Bryn Hughes is one of the well-known sounds of summer in Conwy as he stands on the jetty and calls through his megaphone extolling the virtues of cruising the river in his waterbus *Queen Victoria* and motor launch *Princess Christine.*

Coming from a family that has worked on the river Conwy for 500 years, Bryn did not follow in the footsteps of his forebears when he left school. He became a schoolmaster over the border but the call of the river was strong and soon he was helping his well-known father Rowland sail the *Princess Christine*, and giving an expert commentary on places of interest on the route.

Bryn quickly settled into life in Conwy and, anxious to do his best for the community, became a town councillor and has twice been Mayor.

As he worked the *Princess Christine*, named after his sister, he became concerned that an open boat was no match for our uncertain summers so he and his father bought the waterbus *Queen Victoria*, the name chosen in honour of his daughter. Now passengers are able to enjoy a river cruise no matter how the weather behaves, there are bar facilities and an excellent commentary which is much appreciated by those who want to know more about the history and traditions of the area. Parties and functions and even wedding receptions are held on board and the boat has become very much a part of the local scene.

But there are some people who still prefer an open boat and the *Princess Christine* is now run by Bryn's son Tim who is following in the family tradition and giving visitors an insight into the glorious scenery that is all around them.

Their promise of a trip showing the beauty of the Conwy valley, and the breathtaking vista as the boat nears the open sea with the Great Orme and the Vardre mountain as timeless guardians is a prelude to what becomes a holiday highlight, while their placards stating the times of sailings and that dogs can travel free proclaim to the town that summer has truly arrived.

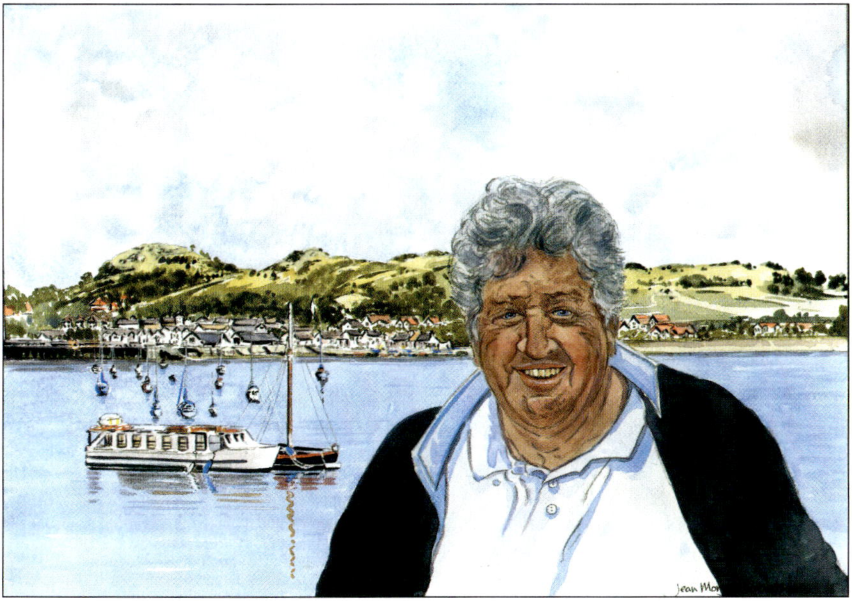

Tony Tobin

Tony Tobin reckons that the most fortunate thing that happened to him was that his family settled in Gyffin almost 70 years ago.

Because of this he enjoyed a wonderful childhood, the memories of which have stayed with him, giving a great sense of belonging.

Although his origins are Irish, he is Welsh speaking and feels a great sense of loyalty to Wales and loves her people. Influenced by these emotions he joined Plaid Cymru 40 years ago.

He was elected to serve as the first Plaid councillor on the old Aberconwy Borough Council in 1987 and now represents Conwy town on the Conwy County Borough Council.

The responsibility of his elected role proves quite stressful at times, especially when trying to strike a balance between seeking development which will improve the quality of life of people, but at the same time endeavouring to protect our beautiful environment, culture and language for the sake of future generations.

But no doubt Tony will take it all in his stride as he has led an interesting and varied life. On leaving Conwy central school he worked at Lewis's Brickworks at Llandudno Junction before serving in the RAF for three years. He then went into construction work. After a short period working with mentally disturbed children he joined the Welsh Ambulance Service and spent 25 years based at Conwy. He flew with the Air Support Unit on 60 shifts and his experience as a paramedic enabled him to carry out voluntary work in west Africa on seven separate occasions, his most recent being in Muzzafrabad, Kashmir, where the resilience and courage of the people in terrible conditions made a great impression.

But he still finds time for exercising his fine tenor voice as a member of the Maelgwn Male Voice Choir.

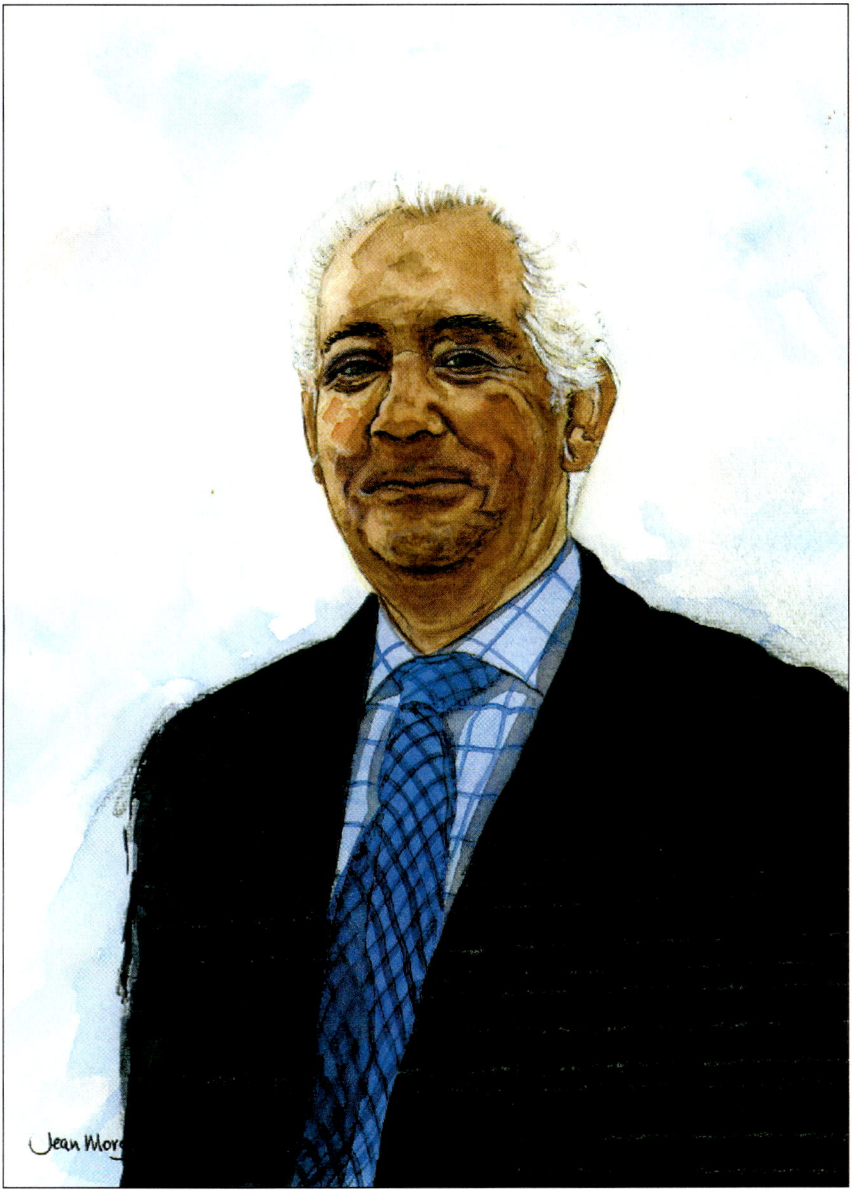
Jean Morg

Lord John Roger Roberts

Lord John Roger Roberts has gone from Llywelyn Street, Conwy to the House of Lords. But in doing so, Roger Roberts has led an exceptionally busy and varied life.

Brought up within the walls of Conwy where he came from one of the town's oldest families, he graduated from the University College of North Wales, Bangor and went on to the Handsworth Methodist College, Birmingham. He was then minister at Aberdaron, Rhydyfoel, Abergele, Llangollen and Llandudno and was the youngest Superintendent Minister in the Methodist church.

Not only has he ministered in Wales. In 2003-4 he was in charge of the Dewi Sant church in Toronto and he has preached and addressed meetings in Australia, New Zealand, the Festival of Wales at San Jose and New York and has organised peace groups and choirs on visits to Jerusalem.

Back home, he has been Methodist Sunday School secretary and Social Responsibility secretary for Wales, has served on various committees and was three times president of the Llandudno Council of Churches.

He is a former borough councillor, was leader of the Lib-Dem group on Aberconwy Borough Council and five times parliamentary candidate for Conwy. For a number of years he was president of the Welsh Liberal Party and the Liberal Democrats. He took his seat in the House of Lords in 2004, is a Lib-Dem whip and spokesman on International Development and Wales.

Roger has broadcast on Welsh and English radio and television, was a presenter of 'Pause for Thought' on BBC Radio 2 and is chairman of the Aberconwy Talking Newspaper.

His wife, Eirlys, a well-known soprano, died in 1995 and his son Gareth was Lib-Dem candidate for Conwy in May 2005.

He is the author of local history pamphlets 'Llandudno and one of its Churches', 'Cip Olwg ar Hanes Llandudno' and was editor of the *Cyhoeddwr*.

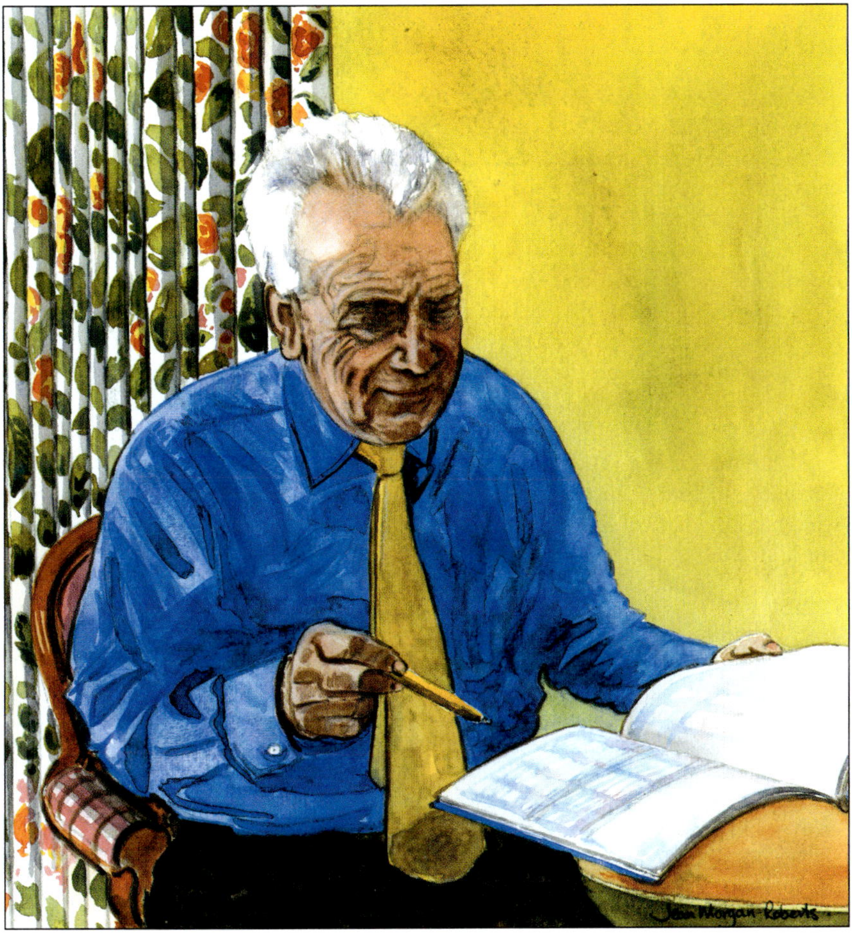
Morgan-Roberts

Lord Roberts of Conwy

Born the second son of a Nonconformist minister and his schoolteacher wife in fairly humble circumstances, Lord Roberts is now a life peer and still humble enough, he hopes.

As a small child in northern Wales in the thirties he sensed the 'gathering storm' and has a vivid memory of the day Britain declared war on Germany and of gas masks, rationing and the death in France of a soldier neighbour.

Towards the end of the war he had the chance of a lifetime when he won a scholarship to Harrow – 'The school that Churchill went to' as his mother described it. He arrived in this totally different world in the summer of 1944 to be greeted by Hitler's flying bombs – 'the doodlebugs' – seeing one stuttering overhead and crashing into a sea of houses in north-west London.

Churchill visited his old school to be cheered by the boys' triumphant rendering of 'Forty Years On' and if these brought a tear or two to his eyes they were well hidden by his horn rimmed glasses, says Lord Roberts, who sang as lustily as the rest.

Called up for National Service at 18, he was posted as a member of the Intelligence Corps to Vienna, already embroiled in the Cold War. Soon he became one of a small group secretly tapping a Russian telephone cable linking the Russian headquarters in the city centre with the East.

This was blown by a mysterious visitor from London. Was it Kim Philby? He tried to recruit Lord Roberts to the Secret Service but he preferred to take up his history scholarship at Oxford.

He quit the ivory towers for newspaper journalism and started as a trainee in crime-ridden, pre-Beatle Liverpool which was the beginning of a zigzag climb to BBC Wales in Cardiff. Then he went to Television Wales and the West (TWW) and became responsible for all the company's productions.

The Fifties and Sixties were a creative period, bringing him into close contact with a host of personalities in the literary world, show business and politics. He filmed an interview with Prime Minister Harold Macmillan on the day in 1961 when Britain landed troops in Kuwait to defend it against Iraq.

When TWW lost its licence to Harlech Television in a pseudo political coup in 1967 he survived the upheaval but was soon looking for pastures new. Being a fairly rare political animal – a Welsh Conservative – he won the marginal Conwy seat from Labour in the June 1970 election. It was the start of a career in the House of Commons that lasted 27 years. He was quickly appointed Parliamentary Private Secretary to Peter Thomas, the new Secretary of State for Wales in Edward Heath's government.

When the Heath government fell in February 1974 he was given a shadow front bench post by Edward Heath, then Leader of the Opposition. He remained on the Conservative front bench for the next 20 years.

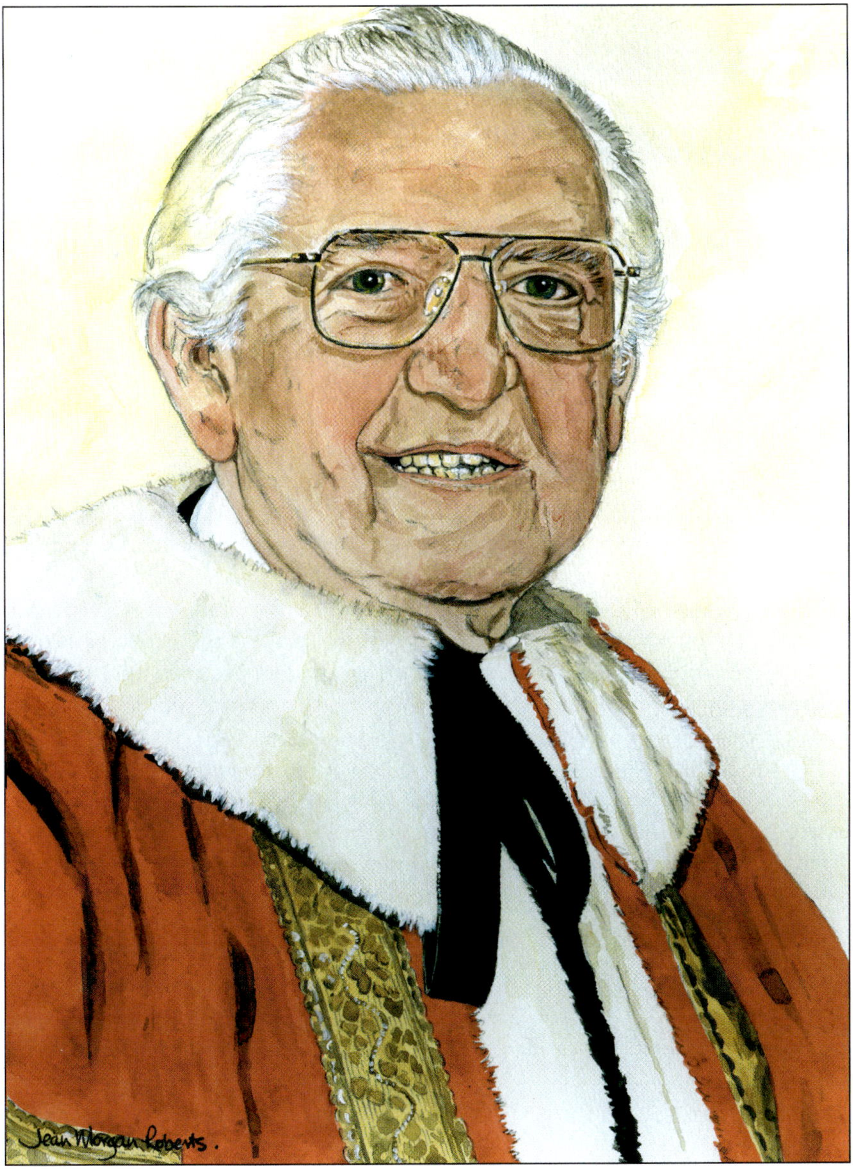

He joined the Welsh Office ministerial team of three and began a record long 15 year stint as a minister in the Welsh Office. In Wales he was dubbed 'the best Secretary of State we never had'.

He was made a Privy Counsellor in 1991 and a life peer in 1997.

Jean Morgan-Roberts

Born within the town walls of Conwy in one of the oldest buildings, the Black Lion, Jean's childhood was idyllic. Here was a garden full of animals – a dog, bantams, hens, ducks and pigeons and lots of places to play hide and seek, while a stone's throw away was the quayside where she spent the summer playing in boats, catching crabs and swimming and Bodlondeb park, a haven for picnics consisting of bottles of water and jam butties.

Jean loved to watch her father draw curlews which flew over the river in the night sky, the moon catching their wings in arrow formation. By the time she was aged 11, she was serious about birds and found Benarth point a great place to see oyster catchers, curlews and herons. Her mother bought her a bird book for her twelfth birthday and from then on she was hooked.

In 1956 her parents divorced and she and her mother left Conwy and lived in some miserable bedsitters and flats in Wallasey and Liverpool. She left school at 15 and became a punch card operator with the Royal Insurance Company.

After the birth of her second child she made up her mind to return to Conwy. She was dabbling with paint, wanted to draw and paint more but never found the time, the money or the nerve to open her own place. Then her work began to be accepted by Medici, New Artist Cards and Judges postcards and she was soon designing greeting and Christmas cards and calendars, and local people began asking her to paint their children, pets and homes.

By the Eighties and Nineties she found herself turning more to painting the beautiful places all around her. She sold her work on the pavement at Rhos Point as well as to local shops and from her own stall at Llangefni and Conwy markets. Then she acquired her own premises in Castle Street, Conwy in 1998, moving to larger premises nearby in 2003, where she continues to paint and sell her work.

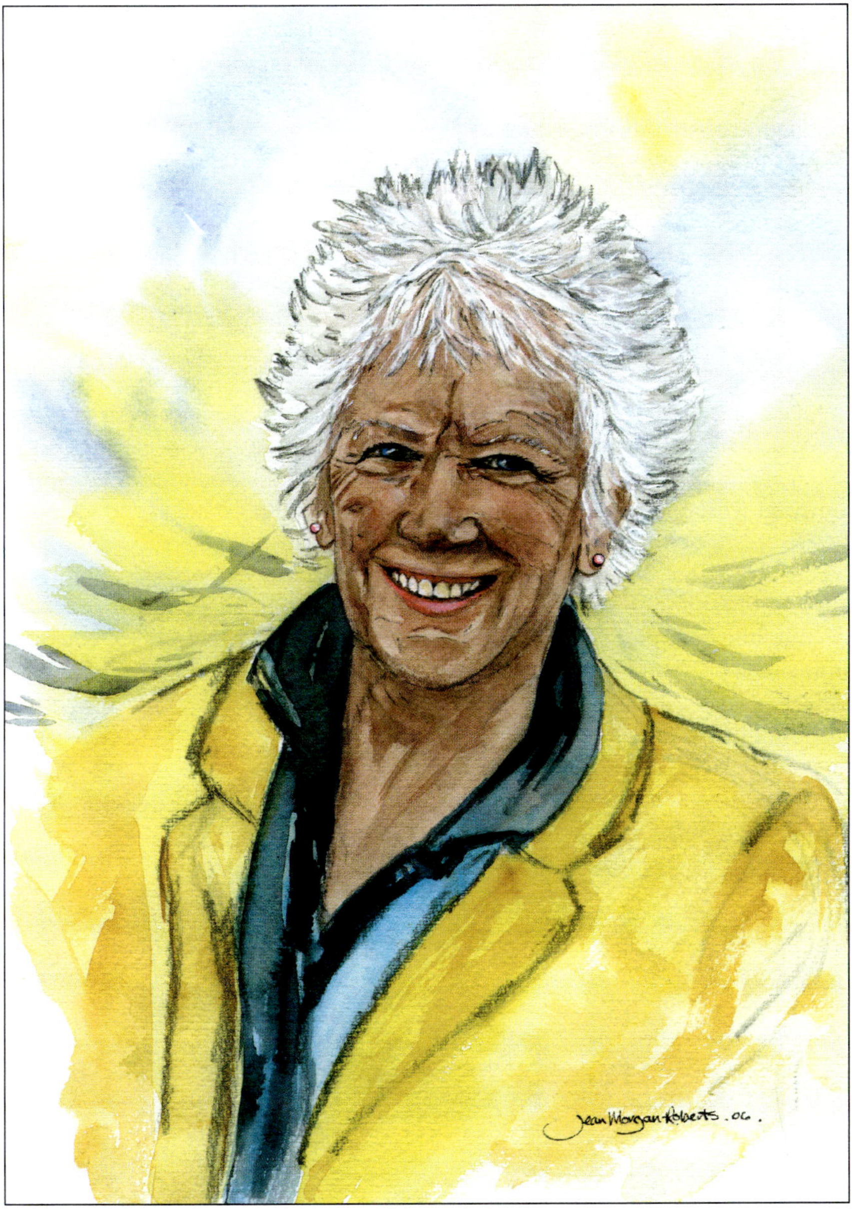
Jean Morgan-Roberts .06.

Jane Hardy

High above the Conwy valley an old stone cottage lies in a fold of the hills. No road reaches its door and few people know it is there. Steeped in antiquity, its great stone buttress leans against the wall, daring it to fall down. Serene and solitary, it remains defiantly intact in a landscape abounding in abandoned ruins.

This is Pen-yr-Allt, the home of Jane Hardy. But she is not a native to this wild and beautiful part of Wales. She grew up during World War II in the East End of London that was all but flattened to rubble by the Blitz. Then she married and moved to Hertfordshire where she taught in a village school for 20 years.

Forty-five years ago she and her husband Andy and two daughters took holidays in a cottage in Dwygyfylchi and one of their favourite walks was to Llangelynnin old church, then having tea at Garnedd Wen, which was a farm and guest house next to the church. Later they bought a parcel of land adjoining Garnedd Wen, and the bonus was that Pen-yr-Allt, a tumbledown cottage with no electricity or water, was included. They spent happy summers there, all fired by the dream that they would renovate their hovel in the hills one day. But Andy died in 1988, his dream unfulfilled.

But little by little, with help from friends, a restored Pen-yr-Allt has emerged from the ancient and primitive ruin. A neat network of handsomely rebuilt dry-stone walls now threads across the fields, water has been piped from the spring into the kitchen and there is a wood stove as well.

Immutable as the timeless landscape, the sheep still graze the land outside and the cottage lives on, bringing happiness to her children and grandchildren and – she fervently hopes – to many more generations to come.

Pen yr Allt

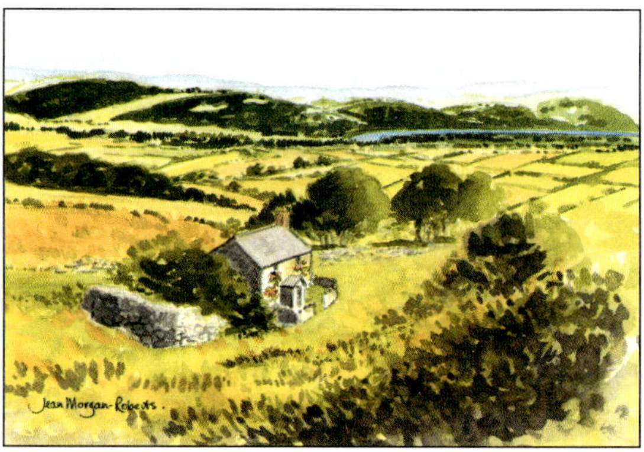

Home to Jane Hardy, this old but beautiful stone cottage stands defiant to time, its views unbeatable.

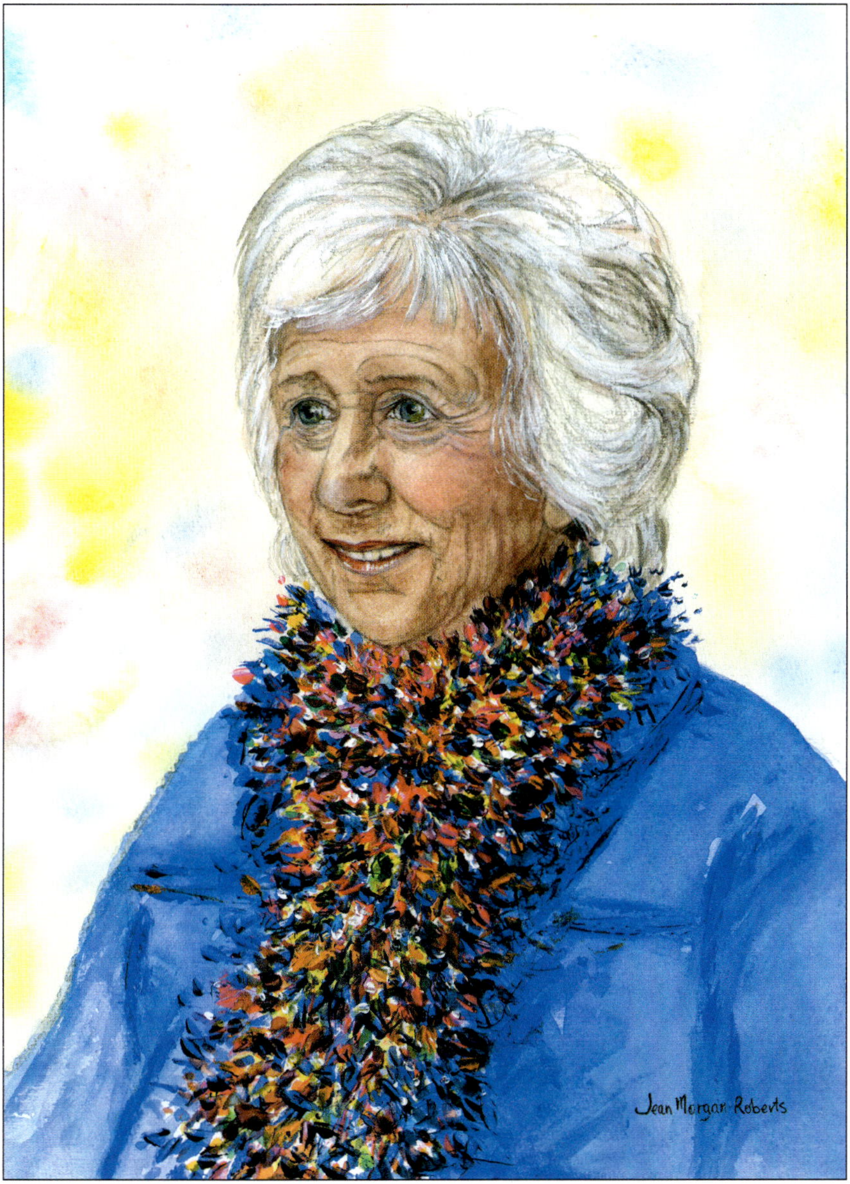
Jean Morgan Roberts

George Edwards

Genial George Edwards, whose off-licence and newsagent's shop in Conwy's Lancaster Square is a village store in the old tradition where people drop in for a chat, is a man of many parts.

A Shropshire lad, he left his village school at 14 and worked in aerodromes near his home until the beginning of the war when he went to enlist, only to be told he was too young at 15. He then became a Bevin Boy in coal mines in South Yorkshire and Lancashire, continuing to work in mines after the cessation of hostilities, was buried in a pit accident, and was unable to work for 18 months. During this time he helped run an Irish dance hall in Manchester – despite his broken leg!

Having had enough of life underground George moved to north Wales to work at the Trawsfynydd power station and he and his wife Marjorie ran a public house at Penrhyndeudraeth. This led to his buying an off-licence and running a wholesale wine and spirit business for 30 years. He and Marjorie moved to Deganwy and they had seven shops in northern Wales, including the one at Conwy.

In his younger days George played for a Coal Board cricket team in Manchester, was keen on darts and boxing and loved gardening. A self-confessed workaholic, he now devotes all his time to the business and his ready wit has endeared him to many over the years.

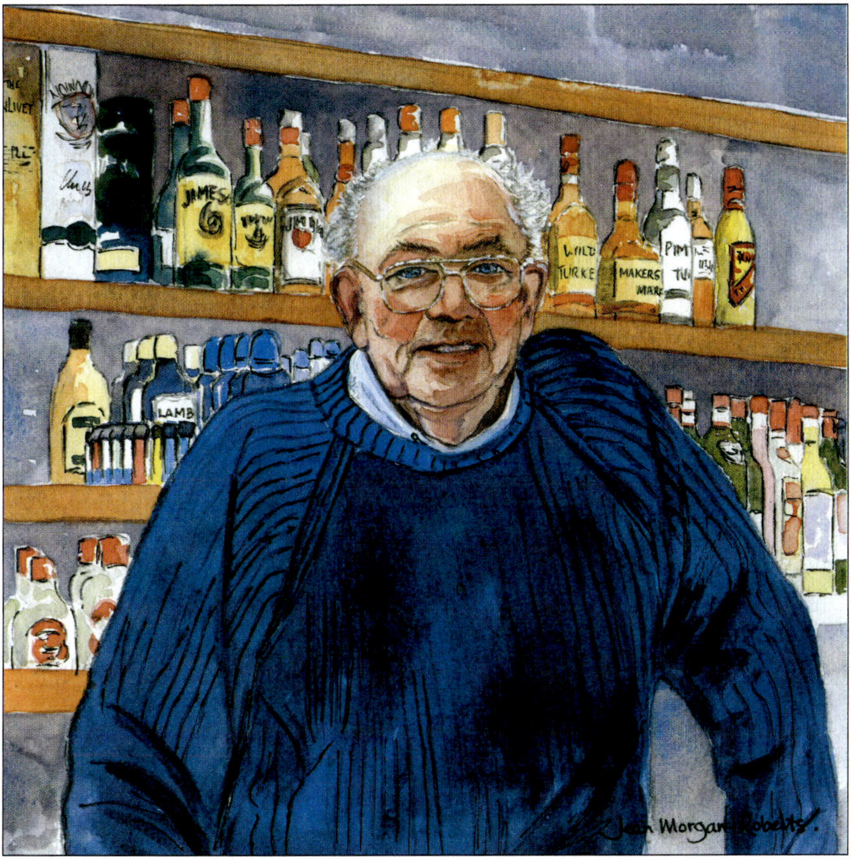
LAMB
MAKERS
Jean Morgan-Roberts

Edward Doylerush

Edward Doylerush has had his head in the clouds since the day he first looked out of the classroom window at Colwyn Bay County School during the war and saw an endless succession of British and American aircraft flying over the sea.

Joining the school unit of the Air Training Corps he learned aircraft recognition, morse code and navigation and had his first flight at RAF Hawarden.

When he registered for National Service in 1946 he was told that aircrew were no longer needed for the RAF and opted for the army instead, served in West Africa and on demobilisation joined the Post Office engineering department.

For a sabbatical he was accepted as a research assistant at Jodrell Bank where he maintained two radars, one detecting previously unknown daylight meteor streams and another detecting occurrences of the aurora borealis even in daylight. He then became an observer for the Aurora Survey for 20 years, climbing onto his cottage chimney with an aerial camera to photograph displays, alerted by activity noted on a simple radio telescope monitoring the sun.

Living within the boundary of the Snowdonia National Park, the Carneddau range beckoned. During a walk in 1977 he came across the wreckage of an Anson on Tal-y-Fan. At that moment he was joined by someone who gave him a list of crashes in Snowdonia compiled by members of the RAF Mountain Rescue team at RAF Valley. He spent eight years researching the subject and tracing survivors around the world, the result being his first book *No Landing Place*, followed by *Fallen Eagles.* Then came *The Legend of Llandwrog*, telling the story of RAF Llandwrog (now Caernarfon airport) and the founding there of the RAF Mountain Rescue Service. *No Landing Place* volume two appeared later. All his books are published by Midland Counties Publications.

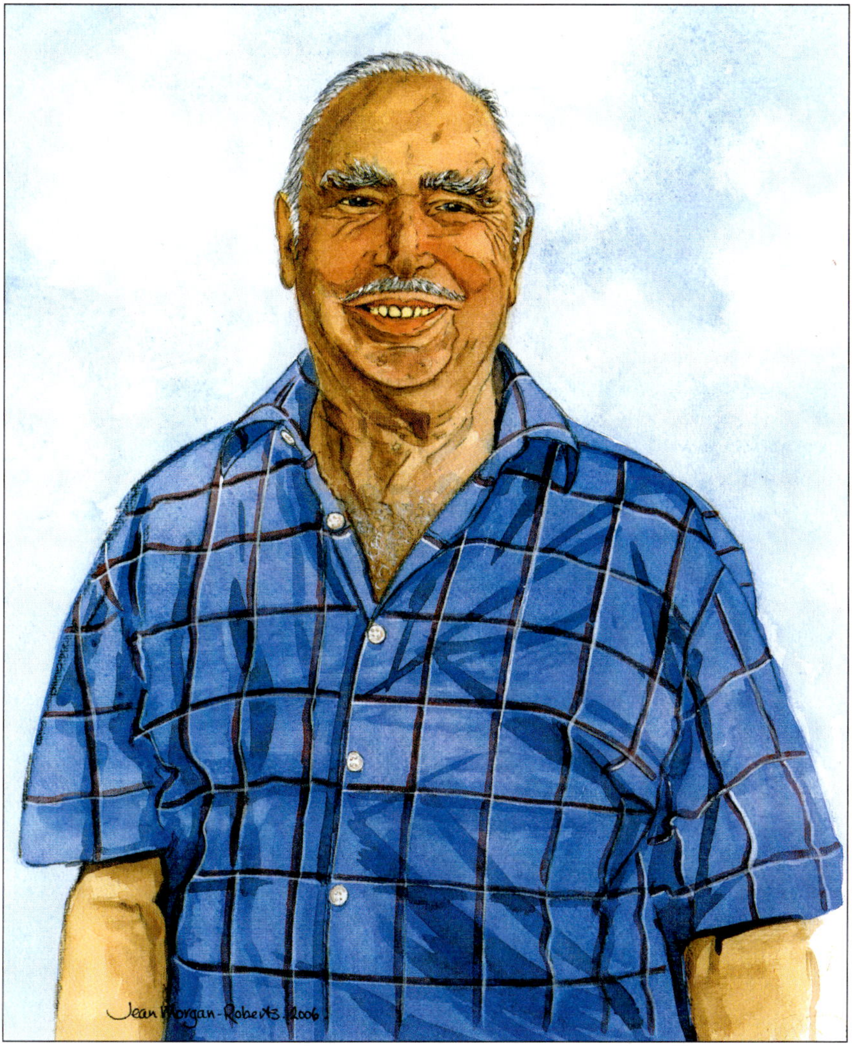
Jean Morgan-Roberts 2006

Dennis Wright

A familiar figure on Conwy quayside, Dennis Wright is at his happiest when he is either sailing or tinkering with boats. It all started years ago when he went to the Boat Show at Earls Court with his brother and promised himself that one day he would have something of his own. At that time he and his wife Enid had a holiday caravan at Eglwysbach and one day, stopping at Woollers filling station they saw a Norwegian varnished dinghy complete with sails and oars. This was their first boat and they used to trail it back and forth from their home in Cheshire.

On his brother's advice and against his own better judgement he bought a boat in Guernsey and set sail for home via Plymouth. The man who helped him, decided he had had enough and as they reached Plymouth left him to complete the journey alone. There had been a gale warning but to his horror this turned into a hurricane with waves hitting him on all three sides. The timbers that the compass was on had been washed overboard and the pump was only screwed on instead of being bolted. This meant he had to spend the entire night with his foot on the pump trying to keep it secure and still pumping water out of the flooded boat. He managed to keep the vessel afloat, find dry clothes and then slept for 24 hours. When he woke he realised he had drifted towards the Irish coast and Fastnet Rock. By chance he found a signal box, pressed the button and soon there was a helicopter above his head and a winch man was dropping towards the deck. He was airlifted to Ireland where he spent the next three days in hospital. He never heard or saw anything of the boat again.

But he was not daunted by his experience. He went on to buy *Ella*, a 30 ft sailing sloop and for nine years he and Enid spent every holiday sailing in the Irish sea and around Anglesey. Then they sold their house in Cheshire and he was able to buy a bigger boat, the *Gay Dolphin*, a 38 ft ketch with the intention of living on board. After four months Enid tired of boat life and they bought a cottage at Llandudno Junction where they still live. Dennis worked at night at Hotpoint which gave him time during the day to convert the *Gay Dolphin* from a master sailor into a real sailing ship and was able to sail her as far as Scotland. Other boats followed including the *Espanola* which was said to have once belonged to the King of Spain. He sailed her to the Outer Hebrides, and to Ireland, averaging 1,000 miles most summers, won prizes at festivals and thoroughly enjoyed his life at sea.

Now retired, he has a fibreglass boat called *Up Spirits* and sailed her from Tynemouth to Conwy in time for the 2005 river festival.

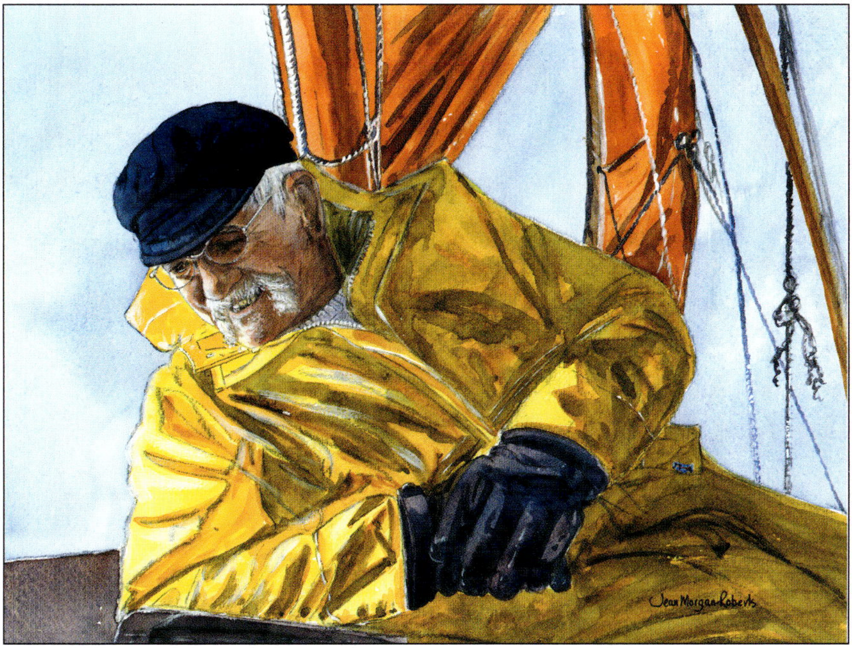
Jean Morgan-Roberts